New Policies for the for the Part-Time and Contingent Workforce

New Policies for the Part-Time and Contingent Workforce

Virginia L. duRivage
Editor

M.E. Sharpe
Armonk, New York
London, England

Copyright © 1992 by M.E. Sharpe, Inc.

All rights reserved. No part of this book may be reproduced in any
form without written permission of the publisher, M.E. Sharpe, Inc.,
80 Business Park Drive, Armonk, New York 10504.

Available in the United Kingdom and Europe from M.E. Sharpe,
Publishers, 3 Henrietta Street, London WC2E 8LU.

Library of Congress Cataloging-in-Publication Data

New policies for the part-time and contingent workforce /
Virginia duRivage, editor.
p. cm
Includes bibliographical references and index.
ISBN 1-56324-164-1.—ISBN 1-56324-165-X (pbk.)
1. Temporary employment—United States. 2. Part-time employment—United States.
3. Labor supply—United States. 4. Manpower policy—United States. 5. United
States—Economic conditions—1981-
I. duRivage, Virginia.
HD5854.2.U6N48 1992
331.25'72—dc20
92-28670
CIP

Printed in the United States of America

The paper used in this publication meets the minimum requirements
of American National Standard for Information Sciences—
Permanence of Paper for Printed Library Materials, ANSI Z39.48-1984.

MV   10   9   8   7   6   5   4   3   2   1

TABLE OF CONTENTS

The suggested citation for this book in the Economic Policy Institute series is as follows:

duRivage, Virginia L., ed. *New Policies for the Part-Time and Contingent Workforce,* Economic Policy Institute series. Armonk: M. E. Sharpe, 1992

Dedication

This book is dedicated to 9 to 5, the National Association of Working Women, for first bringing the alarming realities of part-time and temporary employment to public light.

Acknowledgments

This book began as an idea by Larry Mishel of the Economic Policy Institute and Paul Rupert of New Ways to Work. I am indebted to them for their enthusiasm and their contributions. Thanks also to Jeff Faux for his interest and support. In addition to funding the research in this volume, EPI sponsored a one-day seminar in March 1991 "New Policies for the Part-time and Contingent Workforce," in which researchers and practitioners from labor, government and business reviewed these essays. I would like to acknowledge all of the participants of the EPI seminar for their contributions especially David Jacobs, Meredith Miller, Chris Tilly, Larry Mishel, Paul Rupert, Eileen Appelbaum, Heidi Hartmann, and Edith Rasell. A note of thanks to Ann Rosewater for reviewing early proposals for this project. Financial backing for the book was provided, in part, by the Rosenberg Foundation, New Ways to Work, the Ford Foundation, the American Association of Retired Persons, and the Norman Foundation.

The production of this book required the expertise of several EPI staff. Danielle Currier and Ruth Polk edited earlier versions of the duRivage and Carré chapters. Carol Pott edited the final version and assured consistency in design and lay-out. Amanda Barlow and Stephanie Scott processed "too many" revisions and, together with Chris Timmins, organized the bibliography. A special thanks to Danielle Currier for her hard work and dedication to this project. Finally, I am grateful to the entire support staff of EPI, especially Veronica McDonald, for their assistance and their good humor every time I walked through EPI's door.

The production and coordination of this book was managed by EPI Publications Directors, Danielle M. Currier and Carol E. Pott.

Design and typesetting was handled by Mid-Atlantic/Type 2000, Baltimore, MD.

For additional information on this subject, see *Contingent Work: A Chart Book on Part-Time and Temporary Employment*, an EPI report authored by Polly Callaghan and Heidi Hartmann of the Institute for Women's Policy Research. This report was released at *New Policies for Part-Time & Contingent Workers*, an EPI Conference held on November 18, 1991.

Structural Change and the Growth of Part-Time and Temporary Employment

Eileen Appelbaum

The U.S. employment expansion of the past four decades continued during most of the 1980s, before sputtering to a halt in 1990. But the expansionary gains included a disproportionate increase in the number of part-time and contingent jobs, imposing human costs on workers and forfeiting improvements in the national workforce which directly affect the underlying efficiency and competitiveness of the U.S. economy.

Between 1979 and 1989 employment in the United States increased by about 16 million people. However, one-fourth of this growth occurred in part-time employment. Further, *involuntary* part-time employment accounted for about 40 percent of new part-time jobs. This underlying trend was exacerbated during the recent recession, which began in the summer of 1990. Voluntary part-time employment actually declined during the recession so that involuntary part-time employment accounted for the entire increase between July 1990 and January 1992. The number of people desiring full-time jobs but working part-time because of poor economic conditions rose by 1.5 million workers over that time period. By January 1992, nearly 21 million workers, close to one-fifth of all U.S. workers, were employed part-time.

Employment in the temporary help industry, the most visible subset of the entire casual or contingent workforce, experienced explosive growth during the 1980s. It expanded ten times as fast as overall employment between 1982 and the onset of the recession in 1990. By 1991, tem-

> *The U.S. employment question included a disproportionate increase in the number of part-time and contingent jobs.*

1

porary agencies and employee leasing firms were placing 1.3 million workers daily. Temp agency employment probably accounts for no more than half of all temporary employment. Contingent positions—defined here as jobs in which it is understood from the outset that employment security is strictly limited—include, in addition to most part-time and temporary help, the use of on-call workers, the direct hiring of workers for short-term assignments, the misclassification of employees as independent contractors, and the performance of work on a subcontracted basis. Although it is difficult to measure the precise number of contingent workers because the U.S. Bureau of Labor Statistics (BLS) is not yet geared to counting these workers as a group, it is possible to use available data to develop an estimate of the amount of contingent employment.

Although it is difficult to measure the precise number of contingent workers because the U.S. Bureau of Labor Statistics (BLS) is not yet geared to counting these workers as a group, it is possible to use available data to develop an estimate of the amount of contingent employment. Richard Belous (1989) estimated that the total number of contingent workers in 1988 was between 29.9 and 36.6 million and represented 25–30 percent of the civilian labor force.

This introduction examines the economic climate underlying the growth of part-time and temporary employment and sets the stage for what occupies the remainder of this book—an analysis of the role that changing demographics and workers' needs have played in this process and a discussion of public policy strategies to revitalize the national workforce and protect part-time and contingent workers.

Changing Demographics of the Labor Force

Demographic changes in the labor force—especially the growing employment of women—are often given a prominent role in explanations of the growth of part-time and temporary work in the 1980s. A casual look at the numbers might appear to support such an interpretation. Women and younger workers are overrepresented among both part-time and temporary workers. According to the BLS, nearly 27 percent of women, compared with just over 11 percent of men, worked part-time in 1989. In that same year, approximately 64 percent of teenagers 16 to 19 years

> *The total number of contingent workers in 1988 was between 29.9 and 36.6 million and represented 25–30 percent of the civilian labor force.*

old worked part-time compared with 14 percent of workers aged 20 to 64. According to a 1985 BLS survey on workers in the Temporary Help Supply (THS) industry, women comprised about 64 percent of temporary help employment compared with 45 percent of total employment while young workers 16 to 24 years of age made up 33 percent of temporary help workers compared with 20 percent of all workers.

But appearances are deceptive. In his chapter "Short Hours, Short Shrift," Chris Tilly shows that demographic shifts cannot explain the *increase* in part-time work. While a stable or slightly declining proportion of workers express a desire for part-time employment, the proportion actually working part-time has been growing. Tilly's analysis shows that between 1969 and 1988:

- Nearly three-fourths of the increase in the proportion working part-time has been involuntary part-time employment.
- Men aged 20 to 64 have increased their share of part-time employment.
- Women in the primary childbearing years (22–44) have slightly *decreased* their rate of part-time work.

In analyzing the growth of part-time work, Tilly finds that changes in just the age-gender composition of the labor force between 1969 and 1988 would have resulted in only a slight increase in the share of part-time employment, from 15.5 to 15.9 percent. This is only a small part of the actual increase in the share of part-time employment, which rose to 18.4 percent during this period. Thus, Tilly concludes that "[i]n today's economy, companies are creating part-time jobs even though workers do not want them."

Similarly, Françoise Carré challenges the idea that demographic changes are driving the growth of temporary work. In her chapter "Temporary Employment in the Eighties," Carré argues that recent research on the growth of temp agency employment fails to support the thesis that the boom in temporary employment is a labor supply or worker driven phenomenon. Carré reports that:

- A study examining whether women with family responsibilities were more likely to choose temporary employment found no support for this hypothesis. In fact, there are few statistically significant differences between female THS employees and female employees

Changes in just the age-gender composition of the labor force would have resulted in only a slight increase in the share of part-time employment.

3

in general with respect to marital status, number and age of children, or educational level (Lapidus, 1988).

- A study of the factors driving month-to-month changes in THS employment in the boom years of 1982–1987 found that, everything else equal, an influx into the labor force of women, youth, or older workers has no statistically significant effect on THS employment (Golden and Appelbaum, 1990).

Studies suggest that women are taking the growing number of temp agency jobs because employers are creating more temporary positions and not because temporary employment better meets their flexibility needs.

The results of these studies suggest that women are taking the growing number of temp agency jobs because employers are creating more temporary positions in the fields where women typically work, and not because temporary employment better meets their flexibility needs. Rather it is the lack of bargaining power and limited employment alternatives of these workers that make this managerial strategy possible. For example, firms that plan to rely more heavily on part-time and temporary employees need to find workers who will accept the insecure working conditions typical of such jobs. The problem is especially severe when these jobs require high-level worker skills. One solution, especially in the business services and in the finance and insurance industries, has been to design jobs to appeal to middle-class women by relocating to the suburbs or offering mother's hours. They further target these jobs to utilize skills widely available in the female population—including middle-class social and communications skills and some computer literacy—or require the women to obtain industry-specific skills such as data processing or computer programming before entering the workforce (Christopherson, 1989). The expansion of educational opportunities for women has been a key factor in this regard. As Christopherson observed, "It is doubtful that firms could operate as flexibly as they do if this [female] labor supply had not been created in large numbers by the expansion of educational opportunities in the 1960s and 1970s" (p. 8). Men with these same educational qualifications commonly have more options and do not have to settle for part-time positions. The evidence presented by Tilly and Carré suggests there is no empirical support for the popular view that the expansion of part-time and contingent work is a response to demographic shifts in the labor force or the changing work preferences of female, minority, and younger workers. Carré further notes that the causes for the increase in tem-

porary employment must be sought in the declining importance of internal labor markets or job opportunity structures within the firm (Appelbaum, 1987; Christopherson,
1986); in the demand-side of economic factors including
increased variability in the demand for products and services and increased international competition (Golden and
Appelbaum, 1990); and, finally, in the decline of relative
union bargaining power (Golden and Appelbaum, 1990).

The Changing Nature of the Employment Relationship

From the 1940s to the 1960s the relationship between
employers and employees was fairly stable; employers
wanted a trained, internal labor force and were willing to
invest in it. In the 1970s, however, the inability of U.S.
industries to adapt to the new conditions of the dynamic
marketplace resulted in more turbulent relations between
employers and employees. Increasingly, employers felt that
maintaining an internal labor force hindered rather than
enhanced firm competition and were therefore less willing
to invest in their workers. With this breakdown in the work
environment, employers began turning increasingly
toward a part-time and contingent workforce to meet their
labor needs. To better understand this transformation, it is
helpful to consider the evolution of the post-war employer/
employee relationship and to identify the factors precipitat-
ing the current shift.

The modernization of production in the decades after
1945—based on the application of electromechanical technology to the mass production of standardized products—
yielded improvements in labor productivity that supported
stable, full-time employment and rising real wages in the
core of the U.S. economy. Production was characterized by
large-scale operation and productivity depended mainly
upon the full utilization of capacity—machinery, workers,
and plants. Domination of the domestic market by domestic
oligopolies together with the strength of industrial and
craft unions in the mass production industries yielded two
related outcomes:

   (1) The oligopolies were able to set prices and avoid
      price competition, thereby limiting competition to
      differences in product style. This market environ-
      ment produced a relatively stable profit share which

The inability of U.S. industries to adapt to the new conditions of the dynamic marketplace resulted in more turbulent relations between employers and employees.

5

encouraged further investment in new productive capacity.

(2) The unions were able to negotiate for wage growth in line with average productivity gains in the primary labor market segment. For example, as early as 1948, the United Auto Workers (UAW) won a contract with General Motors (GM) for a 3 percent annual increase in wages for productivity plus an increase for the cost of living. This settlement became a model for wage setting in other union-dominated industries. Stable employment and rising real wages enabled workers in the primary labor market, which includes the unionized mass production industries, to purchase most of the goods and services made available by the growth of productive capacity.

This "social compromise" between firms and workers in the core industries resulted in the sharing of productivity gains from factory automation by both capital and labor. Further, the continued growth of product demand and labor productivity ensured that labor saving automation did not cause massive worker displacement.

Wages and profits, consumption and investment were complementary concepts for growth. Increases in demand and a relatively constant profit share further spurred investment in the mass production industries, while the development of government monetary and fiscal policies, inspired by the Keynesian revolution in economics, stabilized domestic demand. Trade was expanded and conflicts resolved via the Bretton Woods Agreements—a postwar conference on the economy regulating exchange rates and international trade. Internal labor markets provided employment stability and paths within the firm along which workers could obtain training, improve job skills, and advance to higher levels of responsibility. For companies experiencing expansion it made sense to have workers trained and ready to move up the job ladder.

Excluded from this social contract, however, were large numbers of female, black, and other minority workers consigned to low-wage jobs in the secondary labor market (largely outside the union-protected primary sector). These workers continued to be subject to high turnover and competition for their jobs from workers drawn from the external labor market outside the firm. Here, income and employment instability remained the rule.

By the 1970s, factors affecting both workers and employers were changing and the social compromise began to unravel.

By the 1970s, however, factors affecting both workers and employers were changing and the social compromise began to unravel. The average education level of workers rose, making them less willing to accept the fragmentation of work and the arbitrariness of work rules that prevailed in mass production. The maturing of the mass production industries led to the search for new markets beyond national boundaries and an increase in international competition. International price competition among national oligopolies competing for world market share replaced the markup pricing rules and nonprice competition in domestic markets typical of the earlier period. Demand became unstable and the inability of mass production industries to meet these changes became a liability. This was due to the large scale and rigidities of these industries. Excess capacity emerged as a chronic and serious problem. Productivity and real wage growth suffered.

Slower growth in productivity, exacerbated by the oil shock of 1973, had an adverse effect on the social compromise as firms tried to increase profit margins and workers tried to recoup real wage losses. Concurrently, minority workers, inspired by the civil rights movement and, later, the women's movement, began to struggle for a fairer share of the economic pie. All of these factors contributed to the economic stagflation of the 1970s.

Firms producing goods and services traded in world markets or threatened by imports came to view rising wages at home as increasing their costs rather than raising the demand for their products. Many firms sought to respond to the increased instability in demand by firing workers or by varying their hours or work schedules as needed. Anti-union activity became more virulent. The wage structure became increasingly unequal, employment became more precarious, and the number of contingent work arrangements rose.

In the United States, internal labor markets and worker investment lost importance. Firms anticipating a loss of market share or the displacement of workers by labor-saving technology decided that worker training was an unjustifiable expense rather than an investment in the future. *This has occurred despite advances in technology that made possible greater organizational flexibility and improved productivity and competitiveness through the upgrading of worker skills.* The ratios between full-time and part-time jobs shifted as a result of explicit employer

The ratios between full-time and part-time jobs shifted as a result of explicit employer strategies to subcontract work and redesign jobs to be carried out by part-time and temporary workers.

7

strategies to subcontract work and redesign jobs to be carried out by part-time and temporary workers.

By the 1980s, the employer/employee relationship had dramatically changed. As the dollar appreciated, even slow wage growth often failed to improve the competitiveness of firms. Manufacturing employment stagnated or declined. The weak export performance of U.S.-based firms and the entry of foreign firms into domestic markets weakened the position of labor and unions in the industrial heartland. In a last-ditch effort to remain competitive, American firms undermined the wages, health, and pension benefits of workers. With the Reagan Administration's initial success in destroying the air traffic controllers union, union busting and striker replacement became acceptable labor relations techniques, striking the final blow to the social compromise of the previous decades.

Most of the net employment growth during this period occurred in the rapidly developing service sector. Unlike manufacturing, service employment does not uniformly provide job stability, opportunities for advancement, or comparable wage levels. The dualistic nature of employment growth in service industries is captured rather starkly in the contrast between employment in software consulting and managerial services, where jobs have increased most rapidly, and employment in retail trade and janitorial services, where the largest numbers of new jobs have been created. Information- and knowledge-intensive services generated more than nine million jobs between 1973 and 1987 and absorbed more than 5.7 million college graduates at earnings that compare favorably with those in manufacturing. Over the same time period, however, other service industries added 11.2 million jobs, of which 7.7 million (more than two-thirds) were in industries in which median earnings of full-time workers in 1986 were below the median in manufacturing by one-third or more and in which the proportion of part-time jobs ranges from 25 to 40 percent of employment. Thus, much of the employment expansion between 1973 and 1987 was in industries traditionally characterized by jobs offering low wages, few benefits, and part-time hours (Appelbaum and Albin, 1990a; 1990b).

> *Much of the employment expansion between 1973 and 1987 was in industries traditionally characterized by jobs offering low wages, few benefits, and part-time hours.*

8

New Technology and Competitiveness in the Global Market

Even as changing economic conditions revealed the rigidities and limitations of mass production technologies, new process technologies—capable of much greater flexibility in responding to variations in demand or design—were emerging. While transistors and computers were invented in the 1940s, it was only after the development of the integrated circuit in the early 1960s and the microprocessor in the 1980s that the microelectronics revolution took off. The development of information technology made possible a range of new products and services, opened up new possibilities for work organization, and altered the calculus of production in manufacturing and service industries. Small batch production runs have become cost competitive with mass production, making possible smaller, specified runs, thus allowing smaller firms to be market competitors. In addition, smaller runs allow mass production enterprises to be increasingly responsive to variable market demands.

Unfortunately old habits die hard, and the implementation of new technologies has often relied on the obsolete management practices of an earlier era in which productivity gains depended on the fragmentation of tasks and deskilling of labor, as well as the reliance upon machinery for technical skill and control. By falling back on these mass production techniques, managers sacrifice the possibilities for improved product quality and reliability, for learning by doing and cumulative productivity gains, and for internal flexibility in responding to changes in product demand. Instead, they introduce new rigidities when they "dumb down" or de-skill information technology for use by a workforce whose general education and vocational skills managers find suspect. This contrasts, often sharply, with the managerial styles that have developed in other countries and with domestic experiments in which transformations in the organization of work accompany the introduction of new information technologies. In these more favorable circumstances, information technology is used to integrate tasks, increase worker skills and competence, reduce supervision and the machine pacing of work, decentralize decisionmaking, and reduce the layers of management.

The implementation of new technologies has often relied on the obsolete management practices of an earlier era.

9

Management Strategy and Part-Time and Contingent Employment

There is a stark contradiction between improving competitiveness by reducing the size of the full-time, permanent workforce, and an innovative managerial style which utilizes skilled labor.

Employers' responses to changes in technology and economic conditions are one of the primary reasons for the increase in part-time and contingent work. Some firms have responded to greater competition and uncertainty in product markets with strategies that can be characterized as a search for "static" flexibility—the pursuit of "cheap labor and immediate adjustment to changing market conditions" via the destandardization of the terms of employment, making hours of work more flexible and unpredictable, and the "setting of terms and conditions of employment at the level of the individual" (Bosch and Sengenberger, 1989, p. 102). Another reason for the increase in part-time and contingent jobs is the broader range of choices (in the United States, still largely management prerogatives) with respect to labor skills and work organization *within* firms that information technologies make possible. At one end of this spectrum of choices, the robust use of information technology makes possible a strategy of "dynamic" flexibility in which firms employ a highly skilled labor force in an environment conducive to learning-by-doing in order to channel competitive pressures into the product, service, and process innovations that support economic growth (Koppel, Albin, and Appelbaum, 1988). At the other end is "a perpetual temptation ... for enterprises to respond to competition in the short run by cutting labor costs, reducing wages, and exploiting the workforce" (Piore, 1989, p. 58) as well as by using technology to fragment work and reduce firm-specific skills, thus furthering the use of part-time and temporary workers (Albin and Appelbaum, 1988).

There is a stark contradiction between a management strategy designed to improve competitiveness by cutting training costs, reducing the size of the full-time, permanent workforce, reducing worker access to fringe benefits, and driving down wages and living standards and an innovative managerial style which utilizes skilled labor in order to implement best-practice production techniques and gain the full productivity advantages of information technology. These differences among firms can be observed in the relationships among information technology, worker training and skills, worker participation in decisionmaking, and the organization of work.

10

A further important aspect of information technology is that it makes possible new ways of dividing labor among companies and across national borders. The externalization of business services, the reductions in inventories made possible by new linkups between suppliers and producers and between producers and distributors, and the explosive growth of subcontracting relationships are among the most visible manifestations of this development. Between firms, the fundamental question for the 1990s is whether these new and/or expanded relationships will be *collaborative*, with subcontractors employing a sophisticated workforce, receiving financial and technical support, and participating in product and process design; or instead, whether these relationships will involve a *shifting of risks* from large companies to small companies that are required to compete for contracts on the basis of low wages and low prices. The nature of the relationships between large firms and the small firms linked to them by implicit and explicit networks have important implications both for productivity growth and for the skills, wages, and employment security of the workforce.

Relationships between large firms and the small firms linked to them have important implications both for productivity growth and for the skills, wages, and employment security of the workforce.

Small firms that have their own cooperative institutions for doing research, training workers, and marketing services and products to a variety of customers, or have access to research and development and investment in modern technology via long-term contracts with the large customer firms they service, will be able to provide permanent jobs for a skilled labor force (Piore and Sabel, 1984; Best, 1990). There are such flexible specialization experiments underway in the United States, but subcontracting relationships in the United States too often take the form of large customers squeezing their smaller suppliers (Harrison and Kelley, 1991).

Increased uncertainty in product markets has encouraged the shifting of risks and costs downward from larger and stronger U.S. firms to the smaller subcontractors who depend on them, leaving the subcontractors unable to modernize or employ a skilled and well-paid workforce. If this approach continues to dominate large firm/supplier relationships, while at the same time advances in information technology and new sources of competition spur the further decentralization of production, U.S. wages and job security will continue to erode as contingent employment rises. Industrial productivity and the quality of goods and services are likely to suffer as well, over time wiping out any competitive advantage U.S. firms might have initially gained from lower wages. Thus, the nature of the relationship between large companies and their networks of supplier and distributor firms has important implications for whether U.S. growth follows a high-skill, high-productivity trajectory along which wages rise and employment is stable.

Social Policy

The shift toward part-time and contingent work has, in many cases, left workers without health and pension benefits or a living wage.

For too many U.S. workers, part-time or contingent employment has resulted in social and economic insecurity. As Virginia duRivage shows in her chapter, "New Policies for the Part-Time and Contingent Workforce," the shift toward part-time and contingent work has, in many cases, left workers without health and pension benefits or a living wage. Some of the new employment relationships even relieve employers of their obligations under such federal programs as the Occupational Safety and Health Act (OSHA), Unemployment Insurance, the Employment Retirement Income and Security Act (ERISA), and affirmative action. Involuntary part-time employment is often associated with poverty status for the worker and her or his family. Moreover, the access to training, skills, and advancement provided to full-time workers in the primary labor market is generally not available to part-time or contingent workers. The declining importance of promoting from within a firm and the redrawing of the boundaries between primary and secondary labor markets have, to some extent, undermined traditional avenues to job training for U.S. workers. Like the effort to drive down payroll costs, economizing on training for workers is an extremely short-sighted approach for firms to take and one whose negative effects on productivity will become clearer over time.

The ongoing shift in the employment relationship away from permanent full-time jobs and toward part-time or contingent work suggests that the institutional mechanisms through which the United States has met the basic social welfare needs of workers and through which it has provided the skills and training required by a modern, industrial workforce must be reevaluated (Christopherson, 1989). As duRivage notes, "[p]ublic and private employment policies in the United States are designed for full-time workers with permanent attachments to the labor force." After reviewing the social issues inherent in contingent

12

work, she formulates a wide range of public and private policy proposals whose effect would be to provide contingent workers with the types of coverage and protections that many full-time workers already enjoy.

In principle, she advocates a policy framework that provides job training as part of the educational system; that provides social insurance—health care and pensions—as a right of residence rather than a privilege contingent on employment status; that provides all workers the right to representation in decisions affecting hours of work, access to on-the-job training and so on, via unions and, perhaps, workers' committees (works councils); and that introduces parity between workers regardless of their employment status by making labor standards universal. Some of the most important policy changes at the federal level include agreement on a national health care plan, amending equal pay for equal work to include equal hourly pay for contingent workers engaged in the same work as permanent full-time workers, improving pension portability and setting national standards for unemployment insurance coverage so that part-time and contingent workers who lose their jobs qualify. In practice, many valuable smaller steps can be taken in both the private and public sectors such as removing barriers to worker training and advancement based upon job classification, or limiting the use of contingent workers to a small percentage of the firm's total labor force—that will improve the working conditions and living standards of part-time and contingent workers and begin to move these workers into the mainstream.

Improving parity between full-time, permanent workers and those employed on a part-time or contingent basis reduces managerial incentives to sacrifice long-term productivity gains.

Conclusion

Steps such as those suggested by duRivage will reduce employer incentives to increase the use of part-time and contingent workers as part of a misguided managerial strategy to improve competitiveness in global markets by driving down wages and benefits, but it will still allow firms to meet legitimate needs for peak-hour staffing or off-peak use of equipment. Extending labor and social standards to part-time and contingent workers and improving their access to training will raise the quality of the workforce and increase incentives for firms to make greater use of the opportunities for internal flexibility that skilled workers and information technology make possible. Improving parity between full-time, permanent workers and those employed on a part-time or contingent basis reduces managerial incentives to sacrifice long-term productivity gains and reductions in unit labor costs in order to reap immediate but ephemeral reductions in payroll costs. By bringing part-time and contingent workers into the economic mainstream, a better balance between the needs of employers and those of employees will be achieved. The result will be an improvement in the ability of U.S. firms to integrate new work styles and meet the heightened demands of international competition, as well as an improvement in wages and working conditions of workers in part-time or contingent jobs.

Chapter 1

Short Hours, Short Shrift: The Causes and Consequences of Part-Time Employment

Chris Tilly

Introduction[1]

Part-time employment makes up a growing share of jobs in the United States. In 1989 nearly twenty million Americans, or one-fifth of the labor force, were employed part-time. At first glance, this trend might appear to be a benign one: aren't employers simply accommodating the wishes of housewives, students, retirees, and others who prefer short-hour schedules? In actuality, the growth of part-time employment is a danger signal for the U.S. economy. Most part-time jobs are low-wage and low-skill—part of the flood of such jobs that has swept the United States since the early 1970s. Part-time employment has expanded since 1970, not because more workers want these jobs, but because more employers realize the short-term cost-cutting advantages inherent in utilizing part-time work. In fact, *involuntary* part-time workers—part-time workers who would prefer full-time hours—account for almost all of the growth in the part-time share of total U.S. employment since 1970. Ironically, at the same time, a small but significant fraction of full-time workers would *prefer* to work part-time, but are prevented from doing so by employers' unwillingness to grant them schedule flexibility.

Expanding part-time employment is a growing economic problem among working families in America. More family members are working, but the large number of people working part-time jobs earn lower wages and few or no benefits. Involuntary part-time work persists as a form of

> *In 1989 nearly twenty million Americans, or one-fifth of the labor force, were employed part-time.*

hidden unemployment, even when the official unemployment rate falls. And growing part-time employment feeds greater income inequality between low-wage and high-wage workers and their families.

Even for the employers who have promoted it, part-time work is at best a mixed blessing. Service industry employers have used part-time employment to cut their most visible costs: wages and benefits. But, at the same time, they have undermined productivity by moving toward a workforce that is characterized by high turnover, low skill, and minimal job commitment. To some extent, wages and productivity have followed each other in a downward spiral. To shore up American productivity and provide relief for U.S. families, new policies toward part-time work are needed.

> *The number of part-timers as a percentage of the total U.S. labor force increased from 13 percent in 1957 to more than 18 percent in 1989.*

The Part-Time Boom

Part-time workers comprise almost one-fifth of the U.S. workforce. About twenty million people in the nonagricultural workforce worked part-time in 1989,[2] making up 18.1 percent of persons at work. A full 92 percent of these part-timers reported that they *usually* worked part-time. Almost a quarter of the part-time workers—4.7 million people—were involuntary part-time workers who would have preferred a full-time job.[3] These figures represent averages for people working more than twelve months; about twice as many people worked part-time at some time during the year. Since the late 1950s, the number of part-timers as a percentage of the total U.S. labor force increased from 13 percent in 1957 to more than 18 percent in 1989. In the short term, the rate of part-time employment has climbed during economic recessions and dipped during expansions (see Figure 1). But over the long run, increases have exceeded declines, so that on average, the fraction of the workforce employed part-time has grown an estimated 0.19 percentage points per year since the 1950s, rising more rapidly during the 1970s and continuing its growth in the 1980s.

The expansion of part-time employment would appear even more startling if U.S. statistics counted the number of part-time *jobs* rather than the number of *persons* whose total hours worked fall below the full-time threshold.[4] Multiple jobholders—86 percent of whom work twenty-four hours or less on their second jobs—climbed from 4.9 per-

16

FIGURE 1
Part-time as Percent of Those at Work
(Involuntary, Voluntary, Total, 1957-89)

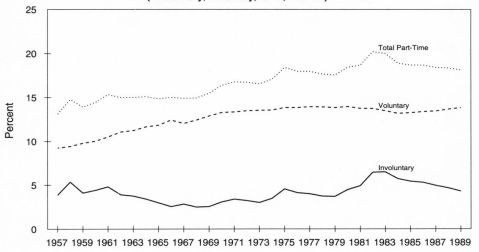

Note: Nonagricultural workers only.
Source: U.S. Bureau of Labor Statistics, Employment and Earnings, various dates.

cent of the workforce in 1979 to a record high of 6.2 percent in 1989, marking an increase in part-time jobs without a corresponding increase in official part-time employment figures (Stinson, 1986; U.S. Department of Labor, 1989b).

Until 1970 the growth in part-time work was driven by expanding voluntary part-time employment, as women and young people desiring part-time hours streamed into the workforce. But since that time, the rate of voluntary part-time employment has stagnated, and the expanding rate of *involuntary* part-time work has propelled more recent growth, accounting for two-thirds of the growth of part-time work between 1969 and 1988. In today's economy, companies are creating part-time jobs even though workers do not want them.

Part-time workers are disproportionately women, teenagers, and persons of retirement age.

Who Works Part-Time and Where?

Part-time workers are disproportionately women, teenagers, and persons of retirement age (see Table 1). Compared to 18 percent of all workers, 27 percent of women work part-time, making women 1.5 times as likely to be

17

TABLE 1
Rate of Part-Time Employment for
Various Nonagricultural Workforce Groups, 1988

Percent of Persons in Group at Work Part-Time:

Total Workforce group	Involuntary	Voluntary	Part-Time
Men	3.9%	7.5%	11.4%
Currently married men	2.6	3.6	6.1
Single (never-married or no longer married) men	6.3	14.3	20.7
Women	5.6	21.2	26.8
Currently married women	4.8	22.6	27.4
Single (never-married or no longer married) women	6.5	19.4	26.0
Age			
Age 16-19	10.5	53.7	64.3
Age 20-64	4.3	10.1	14.3
Age 65 and up	4.5	47.2	51.7
Black	7.2	9.8	17.0
Black men	6.5	6.7	13.2
Black women	7.9	12.8	20.7
White	4.4	14.2	18.5
White men	3.7	7.5	11.1
White women	5.3	22.5	27.7
All	4.7	13.7	18.4

Note: To interpret Table 1, compare the rate of part-time employment in a given group with the rate in the workforce as a whole (bottom row).
Source: U.S. Bureau of Labor Statistics, *Employment and Earnings,* January 1989.

employed part-time as the average workforce member. The teen part-time employment rate is 3.5 times the labor force average while persons aged 65 and over work part-time at 2.8 times the average rate. These probabilities are shaped primarily by the incidence of voluntary part-time employment. Not surprisingly, these three groups in the workforce are those who are most willing to accept lower wages and benefits in order to obtain a satisfactory work schedule.

The rates of involuntary part-time employment tell a somewhat different story. Women, teens, and black work-

18

ers—all of whom already face discrimination in wages and employment—are the groups hardest hit by involuntary part-time employment. While women are more likely to *choose* part-time work, they are also more likely to be *stuck* in part-time jobs against their will. The female rate of involuntary part-time work is 44 percent greater than that for men.

Black workers, while only two-thirds as likely to hold voluntary part-time jobs as whites, are 1.7 times as likely to work part-time involuntarily. Teens are more than twice as likely to work part-time involuntarily as the average, reflecting their weak standing in the labor market, but workers 65 and over have a rate of involuntary part-time employment below the average.

Part-time rates range from 17.5 percent in the South to 20.9 percent in the Midwest. Regional differences, though small, nevertheless reflect the composite effects of disparities in voluntary and involuntary part-time employment. The Northeast, with its relatively tight labor market, has a low rate of involuntary part-time employment—3 percent, compared to more than 5 percent in all other regions. The South and West have low rates of voluntary part-time employment, due both to below-average female labor force participation rates and to low rates of part-time employment among women.

Varieties of Part-Time Work

The categories of voluntary and involuntary part-time work are inadequate to explain why, where, and how part-time employment is used. Instead, part-time work can be broken down into three broad categories: *short-time, secondary* part-time jobs, and *retention* part-time jobs. In the goods-producing industries such as manufacturing, construction, and mining, where male workers predominate, *short-time* is a common form of part-time employment. Instead of laying workers off during a downturn, an employer temporarily reduces workers' hours. When sales revive, the employer typically restores full-time hours. Short-time employment enables employers to keep their workers during slow periods and offers employees an alternative to layoffs. However, short-time is rarely preferred to full-time employment. More than half of part-time employment in the goods producing industries, including short-time, is involuntary, compared to about one-quarter in the economy as a whole.

While women are more likely to choose part-time work, they are also more likely to be stuck in part-time jobs against their will.

Short-time employment, while important in particular industries, comprises less than one-tenth of part-time employment overall. Nearly nine in ten part-time jobs are in the service industries, and in these sectors *secondary* and *retention* part-time employment are most important.

Secondary part-time jobs are marked by low skill, low pay, few fringe benefits, low productivity, and high turnover. Managers who adopt these work schedules cite low compensation and scheduling flexibility as their key advantages. Secondary part-time employment thus represents one form of what labor economists call a *secondary* labor market—a set of jobs characterized by high turnover and little opportunity for advancement.

Retention part-time jobs, on the other hand, are work schedules created to retain (or, in some cases, attract) valued employees whose life circumstances prevent them from working full-time; for example, women with young children. Retention part-time work arrangements tend to be offered only to workers in relatively skilled jobs. Unlike secondary part-time employment, retention part-time work is characterized by high compensation, high productivity, and low turnover—all features of what labor economists call a *primary* labor market. In these jobs, managers accommodate worker preferences as compared to secondary part-time employment where workers seldom have a choice.[5]

Evidence suggests that secondary part-time employment is the more common type of part-time work. Almost two-thirds of all part-timers work in the predominantly low-skill clerical, sales, and service occupations. The data on lower earning and short job tenure associated with part-time work suggest that most of these jobs fit the secondary profile. This is not surprising since employers dedicate entire job categories to secondary part-time employment, whereas they usually negotiate retention part-time work arrangements individually.

The Part-Time Problem

The expansion of part-time employment has serious consequences for U.S. workers. Part-time workers earn lower hourly wages and fringe benefits than do full-timers, and have fewer opportunities for career advancement. To the extent that employers use part-time workers as substitutes for full-time employees, the growth of part-time employment also undermines full-time compensation. Many work-

> Secondary part-time jobs are marked by low skill, low pay, few fringe benefits, low productivity, and high turnover.

20

ers are stuck in involuntary part-time jobs for long periods of time. The families of part-time workers, particularly those of involuntary part-timers, end up with low incomes, a factor that has contributed to the recent growth of income inequality in America. A final, often-overlooked issue is that many full-time workers who would prefer part-time work are denied this option.

Earnings and Family Income

On average, part-time workers earn much less per hour than do full-timers. In 1987, part-timers had a median hourly wage of $4.42, about 60 percent of the full-time median of $7.43, creating a wage differential of 40 percent. The differential was wider for men than for women, 51 percent and 28 percent, respectively. Part-time workers are disproportionately crowded at the very bottom of the wage distribution. Compared to 5 percent of full-time workers, 28 percent of part-time workers earned the minimum wage or less in 1984. Part-timers comprise 65 percent of all people working at or below the minimum wage (Mellor and Haugen, 1986). The discrepancy in weekly wages is, of course, much greater. In 1987, part-timers earned $101 a week at the median, compared to $373 for full-timers.

The wage gap between part-time and full-time workers can be partially explained by other differences. Part-time workers are more concentrated in service employment than are full-time workers, and are more likely to be women, teenagers, and people of retirement age. However, statistical studies controlling for these differences find that a part-time worker, identical to a full-time worker in industry, occupation, sex, age, and other characteristics still earns an average of 10–15 percent less per hour (Owen, 1978 and 1979; Steuernagel and Hilber, 1984; Ehrenberg, Rosenberg, and Li, 1986). This figure probably *under*estimates the effect of part-time status on wages: for example, one could explain the lower average wages of part-time workers in part by the fact that so many of them are concentrated in a low-wage industry such as retail trade. But one could just as easily explain the low wages in the retail trade sector by the fact that so much of the industry is staffed by part-timers!

The spread of part-time employment, which carries with it lower wages, has contributed significantly to growing wage polarization in the United States. Tilly, Bluestone, and Harrison (1986) discovered that 42 percent of the growth

Part-time workers earn lower hourly wages and fringe benefits than do full-timers, and have fewer opportunities for career advancement.

of inequality in annual wages and salaries between 1978 and 1984 could be accounted for by the growth of part-time employment and the widening gap between the earnings of part-time and full-time workers.[6]

The families of part-time workers, and particularly those of involuntary part-timers, are families at economic risk. In the early 1980s (the most recent date for which median income studies are available), part-time workers had a median total family income approximately $5,000 less than the median family income of full-time workers.[7] Involuntary part-timers, in turn, had a median family income totaling $5,000 below that of voluntary part-time workers (Terry, 1981). More current data reveal that about one in six part-time workers—and one in five involuntary part-time workers—has a family income below the poverty level, compared to one in thirty-seven, year-round, full-time workers (Levitan and Conway, 1988).

About one in six part-time workers—and one in five involuntary part-time workers—has a family income below the poverty level.

Part-timers are often supplying a vital income source to their families, yet the low wages they receive sharply limit the assistance they can provide. Most part-time employees (54 percent) are wives and "others" (children and other relatives) in married-couple families. In half a million two-earner families, a spouse's part-time job is the slim margin keeping the family out of poverty (Levitan and Conway, 1988). In addition, one-quarter of part-time workers are household heads. Another 9 percent of part-timers are "other" members of single-parent families.

Benefits

Fringe benefits are not characteristic of part-time employment. Approximately 22 percent of part-time workers receive health insurance as a benefit, compared to 78 percent of full-time workers (Rebitzer and Taylor, 1988). While some part-time workers gain health coverage through their spouses, the Employee Benefits Research Institute estimates that 42 percent of part-timers have no direct or indirect employer-provided health coverage (Chollett, 1984).

Similarly, only 26 percent of part-timers have employer-supplied pension coverage, whereas nearly 60 percent of full-timers enjoy such coverage (Rebitzer and Taylor, 1988). Part-time workers are also about 20 percent less likely than those on full-time schedules to receive any sick leave or paid vacation (Ichniowski and Preston, 1985).

A 1985 survey of 484 medium- to large-sized employers

by Hewitt Associates, a Chicago consulting firm, suggests that benefits coverage drops off sharply as the number of hours worked decreases. For example, 99 percent of the employers surveyed offer health insurance to full-timers, and 73 percent offer this benefit to part-timers working thirty hours or more, but only 13 percent provide health coverage for people working fewer than twenty hours a week. This general pattern is echoed for dental, life, accidental death, dismemberment, and long-term disability insurance, as well as paid sick leave, holidays, and vacation (Worsnop, 1987).

Once more, the question arises: is the fringe benefit differential between part-time and full-time workers due to characteristics of the job, the worker, or the work schedule? Statistical studies do suggest that, all things being equal, a part-time worker is less likely to receive fringe benefits, and a part-time job is less likely to offer them. For example, one study shows that, after controlling for worker and job characteristics, a part-time worker's probability of receiving health insurance is twenty-eight percentage points below that of a full-time worker. Additionally, his or her probability of getting sick leave, paid vacation, or inclusion in a pension plan is lower by 33 percent, 21 percent, and 26 percent, respectively.[8]

Only 26 percent of part-timers have employer-supplied pension coverage, whereas nearly 60 percent of full-timers enjoy such coverage.

Job Tenure and Advancement

Part-time workers keep their jobs for much shorter periods than do full-timers. Currently, the average job tenure of part-time workers is 3.4 years, well below the average of 5.7 years for full-time working women and 8.1 years for full-time working men (Rebitzer and Taylor, 1988). On this basis, part-time workers may resemble contingent workers—workers who are employed on an "as-needed" basis. There is certainly significant overlap between part-time schedules and other contingent work forms—for example, 40 percent of workers in the temporary help supply industry work part-time (Plewes, 1988). In some industries, such as retail trade, employers adjust part-timers' hours upward and downward to meet demand. However, the fact that, on average, part-time workers stay with an employer for more than three years signals that most of them are not, strictly speaking, temporary employees.

Part-time workers are also more likely to be dead-ended in their jobs than are full-time employees. A group of managers surveyed in the late 1970s considered part-time workers "less promotable" than full-time workers (Nollen, Eddy, and Martin, 1978). According to Nine to Five, the National Association of Working Women, company policies often discourage promotion of part-time workers. For example, Control Data Corporation, the University of Cincinnati, Los Angeles Community College, and Cigna Corporation treat their part-time employees' applications for full-time work no differently than applications from outsiders. "Peak-time" work in banks (part-time work matched to busy banking hours) has been designed to exclude job advancement. Says Stuart Martin, the originator of peak-time work:

> Peak-time is not meant to provide job security rights or career mobility. The point is to get workers who want to remain in part-time jobs. (Nine to Five, National Association of Working Women, 1986)

The stunted career paths of many part-time jobs is of particular concern given the disproportionate number of women and minorities working part-time schedules. The growth of part-time employment may significantly inhibit affirmative action objectives.

The stunted career paths of many part-time jobs is of particular concern given the disproportionate number of women and minorities working part-time schedules.

Part-Time Employment Depresses Full-Time Wages and Benefits

Part-time workers can, with varying degrees of difficulty, be used in place of full-time workers. Because this substitution is possible, we would expect the presence of low-paid, part-time workers to depress the wages and benefits of full-time workers in related jobs. In fact, this is true: the higher the fraction of part-time workers in an industry, the lower the wages and benefits paid to full-time workers. Full-time workers employed in a sector where one-third of the workers are part-time earn $1.21 less per hour, on average, than identical full-time workers employed in an industry where there are no part-time workers. Similarly, the probability of receiving health insurance benefits is ten percentage points lower for full-time workers employed in an industry where part-time workers make up one-third of the workforce, while the probability of coverage by a pension plan decreases by seventeen percentage points (Rebitzer, 1987).[9]

The Burden of Involuntary Part-Time Work

As noted above, throughout 1988, an average of five million Americans worked part-time involuntarily. During the 1982–83 recession, the number of people working part-time against their will climbed to six million. If involuntary part-time jobs were transitory, or if average work hours were just a few hours less than full-time hours, there would be less cause for concern. But neither is true. Involuntary part-time employment is, in many cases, a prolonged predicament. In 1985, 38 percent of involuntary part-time workers experienced the problem for fifteen weeks or more—including 19 percent who were involuntarily working part-time for more than twenty-six weeks. In 1987, the average number of hours worked by involuntary part-time workers was 22.1 hours per week, even lower than the average 22.5 hours worked by voluntary part-timers.

Involuntary Full-Time Workers

Despite the fact that there are more than five million part-time workers who would prefer a full-time job, there are also a substantial number of "involuntary *full-time* workers"—people working full-time who would prefer to work part-time. The government collects little data on this group, but it is estimated that nearly three million persons, 7 percent of the full-time workers in nonagricultural industries, belong to this category (Shank, 1986). Another 1.5 million are unemployed workers seeking part-time jobs. The inability to find adequate part-time employment forces these individuals to make unpleasant choices between giving up needed income or sacrificing family or school responsibilities.

Forces Behind the Growth of Part-Time Work: Some Myths

Why has the fraction of the population working part-time continued to grow, even though the fraction of the population who *want* to work part-time has not? And why are there simultaneously large numbers of part-time workers who would prefer full-time jobs and an almost equal number of full-time workers who would prefer part-time schedules? Answering these questions requires a closer look at national trends, industry patterns, and the motivations of individual employers for using part-time employment. A number of possible causes for the continued growth of part-time employment can be eliminated: the increase is *not* explained by demographic shifts in the workforce, by long-term growth in unemployment, or by a widening part-time/full-time wage differential.

Involuntary part-time employment is, in many cases, a prolonged predicament.

25

Demographic Shifts

The demographic explanation for the expansion of part-time employment sounds reasonable enough. Part-time workers in the United States are primarily female, young, or old. Almost two-thirds of part-time workers are women, and another 13 percent are men aged 16–19 or 65 and over. Women with home responsibilities, students, and people of retirement age would, in many cases, be expected to prefer part-time schedules. Consequently, one might try to explain the growth of short-hour work by the continued influx of these groups—especially women—into the workforce.

But the evidence flatly contradicts this explanation. First, in recent years, the increase in the part-time share of total employment is a function of involuntary, not voluntary, part-time employment growth. Second, despite the small fraction of part-time jobs held by men aged 20–64 years old, that share *grew* from 15.8 percent in 1969 to 20.0 percent in 1989, further challenging the notion that the labor supply is stimulating part-time growth. Finally, statistical analysis suggests that changes in the demographics of the workforce account for only one-sixth of the recent growth of part-time employment. If the *rates* of part-time work within each age-gender group in the labor force had remained constant at 1969 levels while the age-gender *composition* of the workforce changed, the rate of part-time employment in 1989 would have risen by less than one-half of a percentage point, from 15.5 to 15.9 percent, instead of actually climbing almost three percentage points to 18.1 percent (see Table 2). The growth of part-time employment since 1970 is mainly due to increases in the rate of part-time work among youths, prime-age men, and elders. Interestingly, women's rate of part-time employment has remained essentially unchanged over this period. In fact, women in their primary child-bearing years (22–44) have slightly *decreased* their rate of part-time employment. Many have shifted to full-time work.

> Changes in the demographics of the workforce account for only one-sixth of the recent growth of part-time employment.

Unemployment

Involuntary part-time employment rates climb in times of high unemployment (see Figure 1). An alternative explanation, then, for the increase in part-time employment is the long-term growth in unemployment rates. However, the statistical evidence undermines this argument. A recent study by Ichniowski and Preston reports that as much as 90

TABLE 2
Age and Gender Composition of the Labor Force
and Rate of Part-Time Employment, 1969, 1979, and 1989

	1969		1979		1988	
	As Percent of At-Work Population	Percent Part-Time	As Percent of At-Work Population	Percent Part-Time	As Percent of At-Work Population	Percent Part-Time
All 16-21	12.8%	40.6%	14.0%	41.7%	10.3%	46.3%
Women 22-44	17.3	22.7	23.1	22.5	27.7	21.9
Women 45-64	13.2	22.5	11.3	24.4	11.6	23.8
Men 22-64	53.2	3.7	48.9	4.8	47.8	6.7
All 65 +	**3.5**	**41.0**	**2.7**	**52.9**	**2.6**	**52.4**
Total	100.0%	15.5%	100.0%	17.6	100.0%	18.1%
Total, holding within-group rate at 1969 levels	—	—	—	16.4%	—	15.9%
Total, holding within-group rate at 1979 levels	—	—	—	—	—	17.0%

Note: Includes only nonagricultural workers at work.
Source: Computed from *Employment and Earnings,* 1970, 1980, and 1990.

percent of the increase in the part-time share of total U.S. employment remains even after controlling for changes in the unemployment rate (Ichniowski and Preston, 1985; see also Ehrenberg, Rosenberg, and Li, 1986). In fact, this analysis suggests that, because of the underlying growth in involuntary part-time employment, unemployment would have to have been less than 1 percent in 1989—rather than the actual 5.3 percent—to bring the rate of involuntary part-time employment down to its 1969 level.

Involuntary part-time employment rates climb in times of high unemployment.

Part-Time/Full-Time Wage Differential
A third argument advanced to explain part-time employment growth is that full-time workers simply "became too expensive," causing employers to substitute part-timers wherever possible. The wage gap between part-time and full-time workers is indeed a substantial one. But the gap has not grown significantly over the last fifteen years. Part-

timers earned hourly wages 61 percent as high as full-timers in 1973 compared to 58 percent in 1989. The part-time/full-time wage differential widened much more among women than men. However, as previously discussed, the rate of part-time employment has not risen among women, only among men. Additional statistical analysis confirms that changes in the wage gap do not account for the recent growth of part-time employment. Nor does the growing cost of fringe benefits (which part-timers are often denied) explain the shift to part-time employment (Tilly, 1991).

The Broader Trend Toward Low-Wage Job Growth

If demographic movements, changes in unemployment, and a widening part-time/full-time wage gap do not provide explanations for the continuing growth of part-time jobs, what does? The answer is twofold. First, the industry composition of employment has shifted away from manufacturing and toward industries such as trade and services that employ large numbers of part-timers. These industries employ so many part-time workers because they are composed predominantly of firms that have adopted a low-wage, low-skill, high turnover employment policy, built in many cases around secondary part-time employment. The second major change is that larger numbers of jobs *within* every industry—including services and trade—have been absorbed into this type of labor market. These structural changes have increased the ranks of part-time workers beyond workers' desires, resulting in the growth of involuntary part-time employment.

Most of the recent growth of part-time work can be traced to sectoral shifts in the economy toward industries dominated by low-wage, part-time employment. Between 1969 and 1989 the shift of jobs toward industries that intensively use part-time workers can account for 2.1 percentage points of the 2.5 percentage point rise in the share of workers employed part-time (see Table 3).[10] In fact, the employment growth in trade and services alone accounts for this 2.1 percentage point increase in the part-time rate. During this period, part-time workers in trade and services rose from 12 to 14 percent of all nonagricultural wage and salary workers. These are the industries where secondary labor markets are particularly prevalent—and where secondary part-time employment is most common. The occu-

> **Most of the recent growth of part-time work can be traced to sectoral shifts in the economy toward industries dominated by low-wage, part-time employment.**

TABLE 3
Industry Composition of the Labor Force
and Rate of Part-Time Employment, 1969, 1979, and 1989

	1969		1979		1988	
	As Percent of At-Work Population	Percent Part-Time	As Percent of At-Work Population	Percent Part-Time	As Percent of At-Work Population	Percent Part-Time
Construction	6.4%	8.6%	6.0%	10.5%	5.9%	10.5%
Durable manufacturing	16.7	3.2	15.3	3.8	12.0	3.9
Nondurable manufacturing	11.4	7.8	9.9	8.6	8.3	8.1
Transport, com., util.	7.2	7.8	7.0	9.0	7.3	8.7
Trade	20.6	26.3	20.7	30.0	21.4	29.7
Finance	5.8	10.5	6.2	11.9	7.1	11.5
Service	24.9	26.2	28.1	25.0	32.1	24.0
Public admin.	6.2	6.2	5.9	6.6	5.3	5.8
Mining	0.8	5.0	1.0	4.0	0.6	4.8
All industries	100.0%	15.5%	100.0%	17.1%	100.0%	17.6%
All industries, holding within-industry rates at 1969 levels	—	—	—	16.2%	—	17.2%
All industries, holding within-industry rates at 1979 levels	—	—	—	—	—	18.1%

Note: Includes only nonagricultural wage and salary workers at work.
Source: Computed from *Employment and Earnings*, 1970, 1980, and 1990. Percent part-time in mining in 1969, which was not published separately, was computed from available information.

pational makeup of part-time job growth confirms this connection. Between 1969 and 1988 part-time employment grew fastest in less-skilled white collar occupations; the number of part-time clerical, sales, and service workers increased from 9.5 to 11.5 percent of all nonfarm workers.

In the most recent decade, the relative growth of trade and services tilted the balance more strongly than ever toward part-time work. Between 1979 and 1989, industry shifts accounted for "more" than the actual increase—1 percentage point, compared to the actual 0.5 percentage point rise—indicating that interindustry employment shifts were offset by other changes, such as demographic shifts (see Table 3).

What accounts for the rapid employment growth in the trade and service industries? The reasons are several. These industries have grown in *relative* terms because the changing international division of labor has increasingly shifted manufacturing to other countries. The *absolute* level of demand for the output of the services and trade industries has expanded in a number of areas. Final demand for consumer services has grown via the commoditization of goods formerly produced at home (e.g., breakfast at McDonald's), in part because women entering the workforce are less able to directly provide many of these services to their families. Intermediate demand for producer services has boomed because of the growing importance of specialized business services (legal advice, advertising, accounting) to commercial success. At the same time, productivity growth in services and trade has been very slow (when positive), so that increases in output have translated directly into increases in employment. And finally, the use of low-cost secondary labor markets has facilitated the growth in consumer demand, enabling employers in these industries to keep prices relatively low despite lags in productivity growth (Waldstein, 1989).

The growth of part-time employment *within* industries, while smaller (in absolute terms) than the sectoral shifts just described, is potentially more provocative, since it reflects not just changes in the composition of output, but changes in firms' behavior and employment strategy. Between 1969 and 1989 the rate of part-time employment in most major industries rose, despite the fact that in many cases, the rate of voluntary part-time employment had *declined* (see Table 4). The major increases in the within-industry rate of part-time employment were complete by 1979.

Firms turn to part-time employment for a variety of reasons. Some companies have simply encountered scheduling problems that can be solved most effectively by using short-hour employees. In other cases, companies have hired part-time workers to undermine unionization. The Wisconsin Physicians' Service, following acrimonious contract negotiations with the United Food and Commercial Workers, rapidly hired 200 part-time and temporary workers and 150 home-based workers. The company excluded these employees from the labor contract, and paid all three groups reduced hourly wages and benefits (Nine to Five, 1986).

But for most companies in the nonmanufacturing industries, where the bulk of part-time employment is located,

> Between 1969 and 1989 the rate of part-time employment in most major industries rose, despite the fact that in many cases, the rate of voluntary part-time employment had declined.

30

TABLE 4
Rate of Involuntary, Voluntary, and Total Part-Time Work by Industry
1969, 1979, and 1989

	Involuntary			Voluntary			Total		
	1969	1979	1989	1969	1979	1989	1969	1979	1989
Construction	4.4%	5.4%	6.1%	4.2%	5.0%	4.4%	8.6%	10.5%	10.5%
Durable manufacturing	1.4	1.5	1.6	1.8	2.3	2.3	3.2	3.8	3.9
Nondurable manufacturing	3.4	3.8	3.4	4.4	4.8	4.7	7.8	8.6	8.1
Transport, com., util.	1.8	2.6	2.7	6.0	6.4	6.0	7.8	9.0	8.7
Trade	2.9	5.4	6.3	23.4	24.5	23.4	26.3	30.0	29.7
Finance	1.0	1.7	1.8	9.5	10.2	9.6	10.5	11.9	11.5
Service	3.1	4.1	4.7	23.1	21.0	19.3	26.2	25.0	24.0
Public admin.	0.8	1.3	0.9	5.4	5.3	4.9	6.2	6.6	5.8
Mining[*]	1.6	2.3	2.5	3.4	1.7	2.3	5.0	4.0	4.8
All industries	2.5	3.6	4.1	13.0	13.5	13.5	15.5	17.1	17.6

"1969" figure for mining is from 1976, because earlier figures are not available in published form.

Note: Includes only nonagricultural wage and salary workers at work.
Source: Computed from *Employment and Earnings,* 1970, 1980, and 1990.

the shift to part-time employment is neither a response to a technical imperative nor an outright antilabor measure. Rather, companies have revamped employment strategies because, in their view, cutting labor costs and enhancing staffing flexibility are more important—at least in some areas of work—than maintaining the productivity and reliability of the labor force. Hiring part-timers is, of course, only one of a number of ways to bring down labor costs. Often companies that choose the part-time route do so because specific scheduling issues favor part-time workers over other low-wage workers.

The retail food industry offers a case in point. In retail as a whole, part-time employment climbed rapidly from 24 percent of the workforce in 1962 to 36 percent in 1987. Among grocery stores in particular, the rate of part-time employment soared even higher, from 35 percent in 1962 to 60 percent in 1985. According to *Progressive Grocer,*

Often companies that choose the part-time route do so because specific scheduling issues favor part-time workers over other low-wage workers.

31

the supermarket industry's main trade publication, grocers expanded part-time employment in search of cheaper labor:

> To cut labor costs by switching to lower-paid part-timers with fewer benefits, the industry's percentage of part-timers has continually grown. (Sansolo, 1987)

The initial impetus for the use of part-time workers in retail food came from the extension of store hours. But then, as one retail union official recalled:

> The retail industry woke up one day. The light bulb went on. They got the profit and loss picture, and started to create more part-time [work] for that reason. This started in the early to mid '50s. Since then, it has grown and grown. In the late '40s, early '50s, the key was flexibility. Since then, the key is cost. (Tilly, 1989)

The spread of part-time employment in the U.S. is part of a broader trend toward more low-paid jobs and slower productivity growth.

Subsequent technological changes have permitted greater boosts in part-time employment in retail food. Supermarket operators have moved toward stores that are larger in both floor size and sales volume. They now maintain a full-time core of department managers and one or two full-timers per department. This core does not grow proportionately with store employment; larger stores have higher rates of part-time employment. Innovations in food processing—such as the introduction of boxed beef—have decreased skill requirements and further shrunk the full-time skilled labor force in supermarkets.

Certain sections of the insurance industry, especially health insurers, have been even more aggressive in building a part-time workforce—particularly among routine clerical work such as claims processing. At two health insurance companies studied by the author, part-time employment skyrocketed from less than 7 percent to more than 24 percent of the workforce in one case, and from 1 to 16 percent in the other—over a period of about five years! Again, labor costs were a major factor. One manager commented, "Our whole drive is to go toward more part-time jobs. It's very cost-effective" (Tilly, 1989).

The computerization of claims processing has facilitated the transition to a part-time workforce within the insurance industry. Automation reduces the skill and training time required for claims processing jobs, while the productivity of workers using video display terminals falls off after four or five hours of work.

In short, secondary part-time employment's share of the total U.S. labor force has expanded due to the growth, in relative terms, of industries that rely on a low-wage, low-skill workforce and the increasing dependence of employers in nearly every industry upon a low-wage, low-skill, and flexible workforce. The spread of part-time employment in the U.S. economy is part of a broader trend toward more low-paid jobs and slower productivity growth.

Why Involuntary Full-Time Workers Can't Get Part-Time Jobs

If employers are anxious to expand part-time employment to cut labor costs, why are there so many involuntary full-time workers—people who would prefer to work part-time, but are not able to obtain part-time hours? The answer lies in the two different labor markets that are involved. Employers are hunting for part-timers in the low-skill jobs that make up secondary labor markets. The involuntary full-timers are those in jobs requiring greater skill, where retention part-time jobs are rationed only to the most deserving employees. Skilled professional, technical, and high-level clerical workers are not going to switch to punching cash registers or doing data entry just to secure part-time hours.

In many cases, it is too costly for employers of more highly-skilled workers to grant them part-time work schedules. Companies often feel obligated to continue offering skilled workers a full benefits package—including fringes such as health insurance that are not easily prorated. Thus, high-level part-timers can be more costly on a per-hour basis than full-time workers. When jobs involve lengthy in-house training, employers want to make use of the trained employee for a full forty-hour week. Part-timers with flexible hours may also be more difficult to manage, particularly when they handle vital information that is unavailable during the hours they are absent.

But managers' resistance to allowing higher-level workers to work part-time also derives from prejudice and fear of the unknown. One insurance manager who has overseen both part-time and full-time workers noted:

> I think you have a tendency to look at a part timer and think of the negatives, and say, Jesus, I've only got him four hours, ... there's a lot more people to deal with,

In many cases, it is too costly for employers of more highly-skilled workers to grant them part-time work schedules.

33

... do I really want to get into those headaches? And I think that might cause some reluctance on the part of line managers. Until they get exposed to it, and learn how to manage those headaches. (Tilly, 1989)

The manager went on to express his belief that the difficulties of managing part-timers are no greater than those of managing full-timers. This observation echoes a survey of managers that showed nonusers of part-time workers imagined numerous disadvantages that users rarely reported (Nollen, Eddy, and Martin, 1978).

Are Employers Really Cutting Costs?

Cost factors have motivated employers to hire more secondary part-time workers, and to limit the number of retention part-time workers. The evidence suggests, however, that such staffing decisions not only have negative effects on workers and their families, but may ultimately be harmful to business.

Employers who hire *secondary* part-timers unquestionably gain lower hourly wage and benefit costs. However, they also find higher turnover, lower productivity, and less employee reliability. These disadvantages emerge not because all part-time workers are inherently bad workers, but because *secondary* part-time employment often attracts less productive and less committed workers (such as teenagers) and encourages more casual attitudes toward work.

The retail food industry—a heavy user of secondary part-time workers—offers dramatic documentation of these trade-offs. The personnel director of one supermarket chain reported that hourly compensation costs for part-time workers amount to about 43 percent of full-time levels. However, the part-time turnover rate in the chain is ten times the full-time rate, prompting one chain store manager to comment, "In my produce department, one good full-timer can do as much work [per hour] as any three part-timers," because of greater experience and knowledge (Tilly, 1989). In fact, at seventeen different retail companies where the author conducted interviews, managers were unanimous in their view that part-time workers in low-level jobs (secondary part-timers) had fewer skills, were less responsible, and left their jobs more quickly than their full-time counterparts (Tilly, 1989). The *Progressive Grocer* echoes these concerns:

> Overall, the rapid growth of secondary part-time employment in the retail sector has been accompanied by falling labor productivity.

34

Some retailers are rethinking the pros and cons of part-timers vs. full-timers. The high turnover rate and costs of training replacement employees may outweigh the advantages of part-timers. These operators point out that full-timers tend to be more loyal and add stability to a store's staff. (*Progressive Grocer,* 1986)

Overall, the rapid growth of secondary part-time employment in the retail sector has been accompanied by falling labor productivity. Between 1967 and 1985, retail productivity fell by an average of 0.1 percent per year (Waldstein, 1989). In food stores, labor productivity plummeted by 12 percent between 1970 and 1982 (Haugen, 1986). Thus, when employers create secondary part-time jobs to cut labor costs, they may not be getting much of a bargain.

On the other hand, employers who bar or limit *retention* part-time employment in upper-level jobs may be *under*-estimating the productivity gains of part-timers in retention part-time jobs. A personnel officer at an insurance company described the benefits of part-time professionals:

You probably will not find more committed employees than your part-time population.... Part-time people will tell you they work much harder than full-time people. . . . They want to do it all. They're driven.

However, she quickly added that in her company, "Traditionally, people have worked full-time, and it's expected" (Tilly, 1989).

Policies for Part-Time Work

Increasing part-time employment gives rise to three key problems: the growth of a low-wage class of jobs, negative effects on productivity growth, and the unique issues raised by involuntary part-time and involuntary full-time work.

The rapidly-growing segment of part-time jobs is made up of low-paid *secondary* part-time jobs. Employer creation of these jobs has outrun the desire for them in the workforce, so that on the margin, involuntary part-time jobs are being created. The spread of poorly compensated part-time jobs also undermines the wages and benefits of full-time workers. Of course, part-time employment *can* take the form of well-compensated, *retention* part-time jobs—but such jobs remain the exception.

Rather than leading to greater efficiency as some business spokespeople have claimed, the growth of part-time employment may have led to decreased efficiency.

The effect of increasing part-time employment on the distribution of family income is more complicated. Most secondary part-time jobs are held by secondary earners—persons who are not the sole support of a family. The growth of part-time work has coincided with the rise of dual-earner families who are working harder to maintain their standard of living.

The problem with secondary part-time jobs is not just low compensation, but low productivity and slow (or even negative) productivity growth. Although conventional economic theory asserts that low productivity leads to low compensation, the causality can also run in the opposite direction: access to labor at low compensation levels makes productivity increases unnecessary for employers. Because many service employers have chosen secondary part-time employment (the low-compensation, low-productivity option) as a means to reduce costs, they may have failed to search for or utilize possibilities to increase productivity that would involve full-time work and higher compensation. In short, rather than leading to greater efficiency as some business spokespeople have claimed, the growth of part-time employment may have led to *decreased* efficiency.

Finally, involuntary part-time and full-time employment pose equity and efficiency problems in their own right. The equity issue is most clear with involuntary part-time workers, who have lost potential income. Black workers, women, and teens—all disadvantaged groups in the labor force—are especially likely to be locked into involuntary part-time jobs. Involuntary *full*-time work, while it does not imply heightened income inequality, does involve inequality of opportunity. Women with young children, people near retirement age, and others for whom working full-time entails significant personal sacrifice are forced to either make that sacrifice or leave their jobs. Involuntary part-time and full-time jobs also hamper economic efficiency. For example, the forgone output and employment represented by five million people underemployed and involuntarily working part-time is equivalent to an additional 2.5 million people unemployed.

Part-time employment is not inherently a negative feature of the labor market. Part-time employment can provide a valuable dimension of flexibility for employers and workers. However, in order to maintain this flexibility while minimizing its associated risks, it will be necessary to

> *Black workers, women, and teens—all disadvantaged groups in the labor force—are especially likely to be locked into involuntary part-time jobs.*

extend protections to these workers, and to widen the government's social safety net.

Public policymakers have made few efforts to address the problems posed by part-time work. An adequate program would address three areas: equal treatment for part-time workers; security and flexibility for part-timers; and the creation of better jobs. Such a program would help to shift part-time workers from second-class to first-class citizenship in the workforce. Policy strategies would be aimed at improving part-time work, not at eliminating it. However, to the extent that employers use part-time employment as a way to take advantage of the lesser protections and limited bargaining power of part-timers, such reforms probably *would* reduce utilization of part-time labor.

Public policymakers have made few efforts to address the problems posed by part-time work.

Equal Treatment of Part-Time Workers

Equal treatment of part-timers requires federal and state initiatives as well as reformed employer practices. Equal treatment, enforced by public policy, is the standard in most of the industrialized world. The International Labour Office (ILO) surveyed legislation and collective bargaining agreements on work schedules, including part-time work, in Western and Eastern Europe, North America, Japan, Australia, and New Zealand. The ILO concluded that:

> A basic principle explicitly included in the legislation in most countries is that terms and conditions of employment should be no less favourable than those of full-time workers, account being taken as appropriate of the shorter hours of work. This principle covers a range of extremely important conditions: hourly wages, holiday entitlements, security of employment, the right to join trade unions and hold trade union office, etc. (International Labour Office, 1986:16)

In the United States, many forms of social insurance tacitly or explicitly discriminate against part-time workers. For example, in most states unemployment insurance requires a minimum earnings threshold that excludes many part-timers. In addition, most state unemployment insurance laws require that recipients be available for full-time work (Pearce, 1985). Social security caps the income amount subject to payroll taxes, so part-time workers (and other workers with low total earnings) are taxed at a higher rate

37

than full-time workers who exceed the cap. These thresholds, caps, and restrictions should be lifted.

In the workplace, equal treatment would start with equal access to benefits. Federal law should ensure that part-time workers receive a benefits package equivalent to that of full-timers, benefits that would be prorated to reflect the differences in hours worked. Section 89 of the Tax Reform Act of 1986 required this, but that section was repealed in 1989 after a concerted employer campaign against it. Legislation recently introduced by Congresswoman Patricia Schroeder (D-CO) would modify the Employee Retirement and Income Security Act (ERISA), which currently requires that all employees working more than 1,000 hours per year (about twenty hours per week) be included in a company's pension plan. ERISA reform should include lowering its minimum hours threshold and extending its scope to other key benefits, particularly health insurance. Proposals should include restrictions on subcontracting for the purpose of avoiding health and pension benefits.

> *In the United States, many forms of social insurance tacitly or explicitly discriminate against part-time workers.*

Equal treatment for part-time workers also requires equal pay for equal work. Where lower hourly wages for part-timers reflect genuinely different job content, the pay differential may be legitimate. But part-time workers should not be paid less per hour simply because of an invidious distinction between full-timers and part-timers performing the same duties. Federal law should affirm and enforce the principle of equal pay for equal work in this area.

More broadly, equal treatment precludes discrimination against part-timers in all areas of work, particularly hiring and promotion. Job requirements may legitimately preclude hiring or promoting someone who can only work part-time. In many cases, however, such a refusal is discriminatory. Furthermore, discrimination against part-timers may mark a veiled form of discrimination against women, youths, or elders—all of whom are particularly likely to prefer part-time schedules. Federal law should protect part-time workers against such employment discrimination.

Enhancing Security and Flexibility

In addition to equal treatment, the variability of part-time employment requires measures to assure part-time workers *security* in key benefits and *flexibility* combining work and family responsibilities. Appropriate policies would address not just the growth of part-time work, but a whole host of labor market changes that have produced a significant group of vulnerable workers: the growth of other flexible work forms such as temporary employment and subcontracting, the expansion of self-employment and small business, and the increased frequency with which workers change jobs or move in and out of the labor force.

A primary measure to increase worker security is universal health insurance. The current system, which assumes that most families will receive health insurance through a steadily employed head, while Medicare and Medicaid take care of the rest, is clearly failing. Recent estimates put the number of uninsured at thirty-seven million. A federally backed program of universal health care coverage could help to fill the gaps and level the inequities in the current system, particularly important for the more than four in ten part-time workers who do not receive health insurance from any employer (Levitan and Conway, 1988). A related reform would be to increase the portability of pensions from one job to another. Part-time workers, who tend to stay in jobs for shorter periods than full-timers, would particularly benefit from such a change.

A primary measure to increase worker security is universal health insurance.

Important measures for worker flexibility would be for the public and private sectors to guarantee parental leave and provide affordable dependent care—including both child and elder care. Parental leave and dependent care would allow primary care-givers, who are also wage earners, to choose more freely between part-time and full-time work, and to more readily combine work with family responsibilities.

Creating Better Jobs

Finally, policy initiatives are needed to direct the economy toward *creating better jobs.* These strategies would help to stem the growth of secondary part-time jobs while also addressing the proliferation of low-paid jobs in the broader economy (Loveman and Tilly, 1988). Other proposals would specifically target the creation of better part-time jobs.

As a first measure to encourage the creation of better jobs, Congress should boost the minimum wage *substantially* and index it to inflation. The minimum wage increase approved by Congress in 1989, after adjusting for inflation, leaves minimum wage recipients far below the wage level they were guaranteed in 1981 and also leaves them vulnerable to future inflation. An equitable increase in the minimum wage would press employers to create more productive and skilled jobs by rendering a low-wage, low-productivity strategy less possible. Part-time workers, who make up 65 percent of all minimum-wage workers, would especially benefit (Mellor and Haugen, 1986).

Congress should also reform the National Labor Relations Act to make it fairer to unions seeking to organize workers. Since the early 1980s, the National Labor Relations Board has upheld many employer actions whose obvious purpose was to obstruct unionization or to weaken unions. Historically, however, unions have been a major force working to eliminate secondary labor markets and improve job quality. Specifically, unions have attempted to extend full-time benefits and protections to part-timers and limit the spread of secondary part-time jobs, especially where they threaten to replace more highly compensated, full-time jobs (Appelbaum and Gregory, 1988). Encouraging unionization holds out the prospect that workers themselves can flexibly negotiate changes in the terms of employment, rather than counting on government policies that are often rigid and difficult to enforce.

The comparison of part-time employment in the United States and Canada suggests that unionization can make a large difference in the status of part-time workers. As it has in the United States, part-time employment in Canada has expanded in recent years. The demographic, industry, and occupation profiles of Canadian part-timers are quite similar to those in the United States. For example, about 78 percent of Canadian part-timers work in trade and services, compared to 80 percent in the United States. However, the part-time/full-time hourly wage differential is much smaller in Canada. Canadian full-timers earned only 21 percent more on average than part-timers in 1981— $8.64 vs. $6.84 an hour—compared to 39 percent more in the United States in the same year.[11] Among unionized Canadian workers, the part-time/full-time wage differential is only 2 percent.[12]

The higher rate of unionization of part-time workers in Canada helps to explain the compressed wage differential. While U.S. part-timers are about one-third as likely as full-timers to be union members, Canadian part-timers are almost half as likely to belong to labor unions as their full-time counterparts. Rates of unionization are in fact higher for both part-time *and* full-time employees in Canada: 18 percent of part-time workers and 40 percent of full-timers in Canada are union members, compared to 7 percent and 20 percent, respectively, in the United States.

As a first measure to encourage the creation of better jobs, Congress should boost the minimum wage substantially and index it to inflation.

40

Policies directed specifically at the creation of retention part-time jobs are also needed. Congress and state legislatures should explore ways to encourage employers to create part-time jobs at technical, professional, and managerial levels. One model is the federal Part-Time Career Act of 1978, which called for the establishment of permanent part-time positions in federal jobs, with goals and timetables. In the two years after the Act took effect, federal permanent part-time jobs increased by 30 percent—some 14,000 jobs. Since 1980, however, budget cutbacks and management resistance have reduced the total by 6,000. The Act built on the examples of state legislation in Massachusetts, Maryland, Wisconsin, and California: as of 1982, twenty-five states had laws facilitating part-time employment for upper-level workers.[13] In a few cases, unions representing public employees, including Service Employees International Union locals in California and Washington, have negotiated quotas for career part-time positions (Sirianni, 1985).

Taken together, these policy recommendations could substantially reshape the way in which companies use part-time employment. Efforts to implement this program can move the United States closer to an economy characterized by high-compensation, high-productivity jobs—both part-time and full-time. They hold the promise that employment flexibility will benefit everyone, transforming the "part-time problem" into the "part-time choice."

Congress and state legislation should explore ways to encourage employers to create part-time jobs at technical, professional, and managerial levels.

Appendix

TABLE A-1
Percent Distribution of Part-time Workers by Sex, Marital Status, Age, and Race

Workforce group	Percent of part-time workers falling in a given group		
	Involuntary	Voluntary	Total PT
By Sex and Marital Status			
Men	46.0%	29.9%	34.4%
Currently married men	19.2	9.1	11.7
Single (never-married or no longer married) men	26.9	20.7	22.3
Women	54.0	70.1	66.0
Currently married women	25.5	41.1	37.1
Single (never-married or no longer married) women	28.5	29.1	28.9
Total	100.0%	100.0%	100.0%
By Age			
Age 16-19	13.4%	23.4%	20.9%
Age 20-64	84.2	67.9	72.0
Age 65 and up	2.4	8.7	7.1
Total	100.0%	100.0%	100.0%
By Race and Sex			
Black	15.8%	7.3%	9.5%
Black men	7.1	2.5	3.7
Black women	8.7	4.8	5.8
White	81.1	89.8	87.5
White men	37.6	26.2	29.1
White women	43.5	63.5	58.4
Other	3.1	2.9	3.0
Other men	1.3	1.2	1.6
Other women	1.8	1.7	1.4
Total	100.0%	100.0%	100.0%

Source: U.S. Bureau of Labor Statistics, **Employment and Earnings**, *January 1989.*

Note: Nonagricultural workers only. Percentages may not total to 100 percent because of rounding.

Endnotes

[1] In addition to the Economic Policy Institute, thanks are due to the Javits Graduate Fellowship Program, the Cuddahy Foundation, and the M.I.T. Department of Economics for partial support for this research. Thomas Nardone of the U.S. Bureau of Labor Statistics generously provided unpublished statistics. Kathleen Christensen and James Rebitzer provided unpublished and hard-to-find research. Larry Mishel and Virginia duRivage offered helpful comments. The views expressed in this paper are those of the author, and do not necessarily reflect the opinions of any of the above institutions or persons.

This chapter was originally published as an Economic Policy Institute report of the same title. The ISBN number is 0-944826-29-6.

[2] In this discussion, the U.S. Bureau of Labor Statistics definition of part-time employment is used. Part-time workers include everybody working less than thirty-five hours per week. Part-time workers are considered involuntary if they report that they are working part-time because of slack work, plant down-time, starting or ending a job during the week they are surveyed, or inability to find a full-time job. Various objections to this definition could be raised: for example, women who work part-time because they are unable to find adequate child care are considered "voluntary" part-timers. However, all available statistics use this definition.

[3] After this paper was written, the economy slipped into recession in late 1990, greatly increasing the number of involuntary part-time workers. Between May 1990 and May 1991, the number of involuntary part-timers increased by about one million.

[4] See note 2.

[5] The distinction between secondary and retention part-time jobs is discussed at much greater length in Tilly (1989).

[6] The figure of 42 percent results from a univariate analysis. The effects of other variables correlated with part-time status may be included in this estimate.

[7] Unpublished finding communicated by James Rebitzer.

[8] Ichniowski and Preston (1985). These estimates control for education, job tenure, work experience, firm size, occupation, union status, and demographic characteristics (race, sex, marital status). Estimates vary depending on the data source. See also Ehrenberg, Rosenberg, and Li (1986), and Blank, (1987).

[9] These differences were estimated controlling for individual variation in age, race, gender, job tenure, union status, establishment size, occupation, and the proportion of women and union members among full-timers in a given industry.

[10] If rates of part-time employment within each industry had remained at 1969 levels but each industry had followed its actual employment growth pattern

since that time, the number of part-time workers would have risen from 15.1 percent of the labor force to 17.2 percent—most of the way toward the actual 1989 level of 17.6 percent. Note that 17.6 percent is the 1989 rate of part-time employment for nonagricultural *wage and salary* workers at work, as opposed to the rate of part-time employment for all nonagricultural workers at work, 18.1 percent, which is cited elsewhere in this paper. This difference appears because of the way the BLS reports data.

Changes in industry composition play an even more important role in explaining the growth of part-time work in the most recent period. If the shift-share is repeated for 1979 and 1988, changes in industry share account for all of the growth of part-time employment.

[11] The two figures are not strictly comparable, because the Canadian figure is based on weighted mean wages while the U.S. figure is based on median wages. This discrepancy means that the difference between the two countries is probably *understated.*

[12] Canadian figures from Commission of Inquiry into Part-Time Work (1983).

[13] For information on the federal Part-Time Career Act, see Kahne (1985) and Bureau of National Affairs (1986). Kornbluh (1988) discusses state legislation as well as the federal Act.

Chapter 2

Temporary Employment in the Eighties

Françoise J. Carré

Introduction

Contingent employment has been on the rise in recent years. Although still accounting for a small share of aggregate employment, contingent employment is clearly affecting an increasing number of workers. We use the term contingent employment to include both employment in the "temp" *(Temporary Help Supply)* industry and arrangements made directly between firms and workers *(direct hires)*, which can either be on-call or short-term assignments.[1] Data collection lags well behind the changing configuration of the workplace. Therefore, while we can infer from micro studies that the direct hiring of temporary workers is on the rise, a national count is still elusive. National data are available on the Temporary Help Supply (THS) industry which places workers on assignments with user firms; they are a reasonable indicator that contingent employment as a whole is on the rise. From 1978 to 1985, the industry grew eight times faster than all nonagricultural industries. Average annual employment in the industry reached 1,031,500 in 1989.

Since the late 1970s, employment practices appear to have changed; contingent arrangements no longer function solely as stop-gap measures but, in a growing number of firms, are fast becoming integral features of personnel management. For this reason, the phenomenon deserves attention from policymakers and worker organizations.

We use the term contingent employment to include both employment in the "temp" industry and arrangements made directly between firms and workers.

45

Data available on temporary employment suggest that women and minority males are the workers most threatened by these employment practices. The existing evidence gives little support to the notion that changes in workforce composition—for example, greater numbers of working mothers—account for the growth of contingent employment. Large numbers of women workers are employed both in the THS industry and as direct hires. Black workers are concentrated in the THS industry as well. Both groups of workers may get stuck in contingent employment. They run the risk of acquiring little on-the-job training and of being unable to move away from jobs which tend to provide lower pay and fewer benefits than regular employment. Moreover, all forms of contingent employment elude Equal Employment Opportunity oversight.

Women and minority males are the workers most threatened by employment practices.

Systematic academic and policy research on contingent employment has been hampered partly by the lack of a comprehensive definition of the phenomenon (Polivka and Nardone, 1989). Employment in the THS industry is easily defined and is monitored by the Bureau of Labor Statistics, although data series include little or no detail on terms and conditions of employment. Direct hires provide a greater challenge. Firms contract directly with workers and may vary greatly in terms of the conditions of employment they offer to their direct hires. Furthermore, firms are not required to report the breakdown of their workforce across "regular" and "contingent" workers. In settings in which even regular employment entails little job and income security, it becomes more difficult to differentiate among groups of workers. Information on direct hires is almost nonexistent outside of case studies (which use different terminology and definitions), one-time surveys, and journalistic accounts. This lack of information is particularly problematic given that estimates on the number of direct hires far surpasses the size of employment in the THS industry. In the future, direct hires should command greater research attention.

What are the potential benefits and risks of contingent employment? Potential benefits include the opportunity to control work hours and work attachments. These constitute advantages only to the extent that they represent genuine choices between several alternatives. Contingent employment endangers economic security when it is the only available job choice and when workers stay in these arrangements for extended periods of time. We do not know the extent of worker choice in accepting contingent employment.[2] We do know that there is a growing need among some workers for varying work schedules and for an attachment to employment which allows career interruptions. The question for policy is whether contingent arrangements as they currently exist meet these needs.

In the current state of employment regulation—which was built around a norm of full-time, full-year employment with a single employer—workers must forgo key elements of social security to obtain the flexibility afforded by temporary employment. In virtually all instances, they must forgo benefits such as health insurance, pension, and on-the-job training. In many instances, their wages are lower than those of regular workers.

This chapter examines current information on temporary employment and its implications for public policy. The first two sections survey existing data on workers and user firm practices in the Temporary Help Service industry and cases of direct hires by firms. The next section analyzes some of the arguments that have been brought forward to explain the growth of contingent employment and, following that, we ask why this phenomenon commands policy attention. We then discuss the current state of employment policy as it affects employment conditions for THS workers and direct hires, and end with concluding remarks.

By 1988 six million persons worked in the temporary industry over the course of a year.

Temporary Help Supply (THS) Employment or "Temping"

During the 1980s, employment in the Temporary Help Supply industry grew significantly faster than employment in other industries (See Table 1). By 1988 the industry employed about one million workers at a given point in time, that is, less than 1 percent of jobs in the U.S. economy.[3] The industry association, however, estimates that six million persons worked in the industry over the course of a year.[4] Average annual employment in the industry grew from 340,000 in 1978 to 695,000 in 1985. This 104 percent increase represents three times the growth rate of the services division as a whole, and eight times the rate for all nonagricultural industries during the same time period.[5]

Employment in the Temporary Help Supply (THS) sector is the most visible form of short-term and temporary employment in the U.S. economy and the one easiest to

TABLE 1
Employment in the Temporary Help Supply Services Industry and in the Services Industries, 1980-1989

(in thousands)

	THS or Personnel SIC	Supply[1]	Services[2]
1980	736	517.9	17,741
1981	736	604.4	18,598
1982	736	557.8	19,001
1983	736	714.4	19,680
1984	7,362	620.5	20,662
1985	7,362	695.9	21,930
1986	7,362	786.9	23,072
1987	7,362	944.3	24,137
1988	7,362	1,015.8	25,464
1989	7,362	1,031.5	26,892

[1] Prior to 1984, published data only provide employment levels for the broader industry SIC 736, Personnel Supply Services, 75 percent of whose employment is estimated to be in the THS industry.
[2] Services division: hotels, personal services, business services, repair services, entertainment, health services, legal and social services, and membership organizations.
Source: U.S. Department of Labor, Bureau of Labor Statistics, *Employment and Earnings,* March of 1981-90, Table B2, Washington, DC: USGPO, 1981-90. Establishment data, not seasonally adjusted, employees on nonagricultural payrolls.

monitor because it constitutes a separate industry (DOL Standard Industry Classification SIC 7362). The services which the industry provides allow user firms to externalize workers. The THS worker is on the payroll of the THS agency but is assigned to, and supervised by, the user firm. The THS agency charges a fee for the worker's services; the worker receives a portion of this fee as wage. Even though the employee is working at the customer's site, the THS agency has responsibility as an employer. THS firms hire and fire, issue paychecks, withhold payroll taxes, and make required employer contributions for Unemployment Insurance, Worker's Compensation, and Social Security (Carey and Hazelbaker, 1986, p. 29).

While the first THS firms in the United States opened in the 1940s, it is only since the 1970s, as the industry size expanded, that their activities have become a source of policy concern. Moreover, industry employment has become less cyclical; it did not fall as fast during the early recession of the 1980s as it did in previous recessions (Hartmann and Lapidus, 1989). Employment in the THS industry declined by 18 percent in 1971 and 26 percent in 1975 yet declined by only 5 percent during the severe recessions of the early 1980s (Hartmann and Lapidus, 1989, p. 10). This phenomenon is an indication that the use of THS workers may have become an integral part of personnel management in a number of firms. Employment in the industry had previously consisted of "stop-gap" assignments of short duration with little employment continuity. Reports indicate that in an increasing number of cases, temporary workers end up working fulltime, over long stretches of time, and for the same user firm. It is not unusual for individual assignments to last weeks and even months (Plewes, 1988). It is this shift from supplying stop-gap employees to taking over the payroll of entire departments such as mail room facilities[6] that suggests that the industry's growth in the 1980s is not only related to changes in the business cycle but may also reflect structural changes in employment practices on the part of firms that use THS workers.

The use of THS workers may have become an integral part of personnel management in a number of firms.

The rapid growth and increasing "integration" of THS assignments in employment structures raise questions about the extent of worker choice in THS employment and the motivations of firms who use those workers. Do workers choose full-time THS employment because it allows for job hopping? Do they work in the industry because they want part-time employment and the industry offers numerous part-time assignments? Or do these choices reflect the inability to secure more permanent part-time or full-time positions? Unlike the Bureau of Labor Statistics (BLS) data on part-time work which provides information on involuntary part-time employment, no national survey question asks THS workers whether they work in the THS industry because they cannot find regular work. This question becomes particularly salient in the case of those THS workers in long-duration assignments with the same user firm. Do employers use THS workers as a "just-in-time" workforce to minimize labor costs and reduce regular employment? (Belous, 1989b, p. 32). Some labor market analysts have noted that 55 percent of the growth of producer services employment between 1972 and 1985 was due to changes in business practices.[7]

Characteristics of THS Workers

In May 1985, the Current Population Survey (CPS) counted 455,000 persons who viewed their jobs as temporary and whose salaries were paid by a THS agency.[8] This is noticeably smaller than the 695,000 employment figure reported by the 1985 establishment survey—which also includes the permanent staff of agencies (Current Employment Statistics). The CPS probably provides an undercount; it excludes many THS workers who do not view their jobs as temporary because they have a fairly continuous attachment to the THS agency for which they work (Howe, 1986b).

To date, the May 1985 CPS is our only source of systematic information on THS workers. It provides one-time data but the profile of THS workers which it yields mirrors some of the earlier evidence from small-scale surveys and case studies.[9]

THS workers are disproportionately female, young, and black (see Table 2). Women account for 64.2 percent of THS employees, as opposed to 45 percent of workers in all industries. Members of the sixteen to twenty-four-year-old age group represent one out of three temp workers as compared to one out of five workers in all industries. Members of the twenty-five to fifty-four and fifty-five-plus age groups are less represented among temp workers than in the total employed workforce.

Black workers constitute 20.2 percent of temp employees versus 10.4 percent of the workforce in all industries. The group of occupations in which black workers are concentrated in THS employment mirrors the occupations in which black workers are concentrated in all industries. These occupations tend to cluster in the THS industry, thus accounting for the relative overrepresentation of black workers in the industry. There is even a striking similarity in gender distribution. Black men account for 48.9 percent of black temp workers compared to 49.4 percent of black workers in all industries. The same holds true for black women who represent 51.1 percent of black temp workers, and 50.6 percent of black workers in all industries. This parallelism does not hold for the white workforce; as noted, white women are overrepresented in the industry as compared to their share of the workforce in all industries.

Arguments that contend that THS employment has grown because it meets the specific needs and choices of certain categories of workers—young workers and women who need to combine family and work responsibilities—are insufficient to explain the concentration of black work-

Women account for 64.2 percent of THS employees, as opposed to 45 percent of workers in all industries.

50

TABLE 2
Employed Wage and Salary Workers in All Industries and in the THS Industry, by Selected Characteristics, May 1985

	Percent Distribution	
	All Industries	THS Industry
Age		
Total, 16 yrs and over	100.0%	100.0%
16 to 24	20.1	32.7
25 to 54	67.4	57.6
55 and over	12.5	9.7
Sex and race		
Men	55.0	35.8
Women	45.0	64.2
White	86.9	75.4
Black	10.4	20.2
White	100.0	100.0
White men	55.7	33.2
White women	44.3	66.8
Black	100.0	100.0
Black men	49.4	48.9
Black women	50.6	51.1
Occupations		
Managerial and professional specialty	24.0	11.0
Technical, sales, and administrative support	31.6	52.1
Administrative support, including clerical	17.3	43.3
Service occupations	13.7	10.8
Precision production, craft, and repair	12.1	4.6
Operators, fabricators, and laborers	16.6	16.9
Farming, forestry, and fishing	2.1	4.4

Source: Howe, 1986.

ers, regardless of gender, in THS employment. For black workers, any explanation has to include a comparison of the structure of employment opportunities both in the economy as a whole and in the THS industry. As will be discussed later, research also provides little support for the notion that women are concentrated in the industry because of their specific work and family needs.

Work Hours of THS Workers

How should we think about THS jobs? If we view the main appeal of THS employment as offering shorter weekly hours, then the finding that the vast majority (60 percent) of THS workers work full-time schedules runs counter to our expectations. If, on the other hand, we view THS employment as a substitute for full-time employment, then the presence of 40 percent of part-timers in the industry is worrisome because it raises the strong possibility that workers looking for full-time work have a greater likelihood of working involuntary part-time schedules than workers in the economy at large. Data on weeks worked per year (which are not yet available) would document the extent of part-year employment in the industry and provide another measure of the industry's degree of employment stability. It is likely that a large number of temp jobs involve full-time schedules but part-year employment.

Detailed evidence from the May 1985 CPS suggest that THS employees are twice as likely to work part-time as workers in the economy as a whole (see Table 3): 40 percent have part-time schedules (compared with 19 percent in the total workforce) but details on average work hours are unavailable. Men in the industry are more likely to work full-time than women—64.4 percent of male workers work full-time compared with 57.5 percent of female workers. As in all industries, marital status affects women's employment experience; 50.7 percent of married women with a husband present worked full-time in the THS industry, compared with 64.9 percent of single women in the industry.

Within the THS industry, black workers are more likely to work part-time. More than half of black workers in the industry (55.3 percent) work part-time compared with an overall THS industry part-time rate of 40 percent. This variation across racial groups is particularly troublesome because there is no evidence suggesting that black THS workers have a greater need for part-time schedules than other workers in the industry.

TABLE 3
Employed Full- and Part-time Wage and Salary Workers in the THS Industry, by Selected Characteristics, May 1985

	Percent Distribution	
	Full-time Workers	Part-time Workers
Age		
Total, 16 yrs and over	60.0%	40.0%
16 to 24	55.7	44.3
25 to 54	66.8	33.2
55 and over[1]		
Sex and race		
Men	64.4	35.6
Women[2]	57.5	42.5
Single	64.9	35.1
Married, spouse present	50.7	49.3
White	62.7	37.3
White men	71.0	29.0
White women	58.5	41.5
Black	44.6	55.3
Black men[1]		
Black women[1]		
Occupations		
Technical, sales, and administrative support	66.1	33.9
Administrative support, including clerical	66.6	33.4
Operators, fabricators, and laborers	55.3	44.7
All other occupations	51.8	48.2

[1] Data not shown where base is less than 75,000.
[2] Includes widowed, divorced, and separated women, not shown separately.
Source: Howe, 1986.

Administrative support occupations account for 43.3 percent of THS workers and include all clerical occupations such as office clerks, secretaries, typists, and receptionists, hence the image of the "temp" female secretary. This concentration of clerical occupations is two-and-a-half times greater than that in all industries. Administrative support occupations belong to the broader category of technical, sales, and administrative support occupations which account for the majority (52.1 percent) of THS employment.

Among the THS industry's biggest occupations, women are more likely to work full-time than are male workers— reversing employment patterns for the total workforce. Clerical jobs, which constitute the single largest job group, are predominantly female and full-time, while industrial jobs, which comprise the second largest category, are predominantly male and part-time. In the larger economy, 80 percent of these workers have full-time schedules (see Table 4). Within the THS industry's total workforce, clerical workers are more likely to work full-time—66.6 percent have full-time schedules—compared with 60 percent for the industry as a whole. The demand for these clerical occupations is less sensitive to cyclical and seasonal changes than that for industrial workers (and for engineering and technical workers).

Industrial help workers, operators, fabricators, and laborers are the second largest worker group in the THS industry, representing 16.9 percent of all THS workers. Almost 90 percent of these workers are men and a disproportionate number are black. When compared with clerical workers in the THS industry, fewer of these workers are likely to work full-time. Only 55.3 percent of operators have full-time schedules compared with 66.6 percent of clerical workers. In the overall economy, 83.8 percent of industrial help work is full-time compared with 80 percent of total clerical employment (Howe, 1986b, p. 47).

Plewes (1988) argues that the wide availability of casual manual labor is partly responsible for the large representation of black workers in the industry. Black men in particular are more likely to be employed in these jobs in the economy as a whole than their white counterparts. For instance, in May 1985, industrial help occupations accounted for 32.7 percent of total black male employment in all industries as compared to only 19.8 percent of total white male employment.[10]

Administrative support occupations account for the majority (52.1 percent) of THS employment.

TABLE 4
Employed Full- and Part-time Wage and Salary Workers in All Industries, by Selected Characteristics, May 1985

	Percent Distribution	
	Full-time Workers	Part-time Workers
Age		
Total, 16 yrs and over	80.9%	19.1%
16 to 24	63.0	37.0
25 to 54	87.0	13.0
55 and over	75.3	24.7
Sex and race		
Men	88.0	11.9
Women	71.8	28.2
White		
White men	88.4	11.6
White women	70.8	29.2
Black		
Black men	84.1	15.9
Black women	77.7	22.2
Occupations[1]		
Technical, sales, and administrative support	78.9	21.1
Administrative support, including clerical	80.4	18.7
Operators, fabricators, and laborers	83.8	16.2

[1] Data concern people at work during survey week.
Source: Computations with data from U.S. Department Of Labor, Bureau of Labor Statistics, *Employment and Earnings,* June 1985, Tables A9 and A31. Data are household data, not seasonally adjusted.

The third largest occupational groups in the THS industry are managerial and professional occupations (such as accountants, programmers, draftsmen) and services occupations (such as security guards, home health aides, and nurses aides). These categories account for 11 percent and 10.8 percent, respectively, of all THS employment.

Wages of THS Workers

On average, THS workers earn less than workers in the economy as a whole. A Bureau of Labor Statistics survey conducted in September 1987 provides limited information on wages and benefits in the THS industry.[11] The average wage for the THS industry's workforce was $6.42 per hour, but hourly wages for individual workers ranged from the federal minimum of $3.35 to $20 or more (see Table 5).[12] Based on the May 1985 CPS, Lapidus (1989) calculated that women THS workers earned $5.92 per hour as compared to $5.96 an hour for a random sample of all women workers. Male THS workers earned much less on average than a random sample of male workers; $5.39 per hour as compared to $10.02 per hour (Hartmann and Lapidus, 1989, p. 22). Thus the "cost" of being a THS worker is much greater for male than female workers, suggesting further that THS jobs for female workers mirror their job opportunities in the economy at large (meaning they receive low wages at all levels), whereas THS employment for males represents a subset of inadequate jobs paying hourly wages less than the average hourly earnings of women in the industry.

Benefit Coverage for THS Workers

It is often said that temp workers do not need job-related health benefits because they obtain them from another source, usually a spouse. However, the Employee Benefits Research Institute estimates that, in 1985, 30 percent of temporary employees were without health insurance, whether provided through a job or a spouse, and 63 percent had no employer-sponsored pension plan (Dillon, 1987, p. 49).

The September 1987 BLS survey counts the proportion of temp workers employed by establishments providing specified benefit plans, but does not provide information on the share of these workers who met benefit eligibility requirements (e.g., minimum number of hours worked) and actually received these benefits.[13] Thus the information presented below must be interpreted with caution.

TABLE 5
Employment and Average Wages for Temp Workers in the Temporary Help Service Industry, September 1987

	Number	Percent	Hourly Wage
All Temporary Workers	628,592	100.00%	$6.42
Executive, administrative, and managerial	2,483	0.39	12.31
Professional specialty	20,653	3.28	16.96
Technical and related support	24,301	3.86	11.02
Sales and marketing	9,744	1.55	5.39
Administrative support	328,828	52.31	6.46
Service[1]	46,347	7.37	5.13
Precision, production, craft, and repair	7,708	1.23	8.14
Operators, fabricators, and laborers	160,631	25.55	4.65

[1] Of these, 22,964 are nurses' aides, orderlies, and attendants.
Note: Data do not include the permanent staff employed by THS agencies.
Source: Williams, 1989, p. 4.

Nearly three-fourths of THS workers work in establishments that provide no health benefits. Where health insurance is available, coverage is limited. While most establishments that offer health benefits allow workers with fewer than 500 hours of work a year to participate, eligibility requirements for maintaining this coverage often mandate that the temporary employee work a minimum number of hours per month. Such plans rarely involve any employer subsidy of the health care insurance premium (Nine to Five, 1986, p. 22). A company-run survey of 20,000 Manpower, Inc. employees reports that fewer than 23 percent of its workers were even eligible for the company's health plan, yet only 35 percent of this group actually enrolled in it. A majority of those eligible reported having health coverage through parents, spouse, school, or continuing coverage from a previous employer (Fromstein, 1988, p. 111), arrangements which suggest only temporary solutions to serious coverage gaps.

Nearly three-fourths of THS workers work in establishments that provide no health benefits.

About 75 percent of temporary employees work for THS services which provide vacation pay. Most workers qualify for one week of paid vacation if they work 1,500 hours yearly. Two-fifths receive two weeks paid vacation if they work over 2,000 hours per year (an amount equivalent to full-time work fifty weeks per year). In addition, two-fifths of temps work for establishments that offer paid holidays (about six days per year).

A number of other benefits that THS firms provide are tied to the operation of the industry rather than to worker needs. Three-fifths of temporary workers can earn referral bonuses by recruiting new hires willing to work for a specified period of time (U.S. Department of Labor, 1988c). About one-fourth work for establishments that provide free transportation or cash allowances for job-related travel. The occupational groups most likely to receive these allowances are laborers (transportation to a construction site) and home-care workers. Finally, just over half of THS workers work for establishments that provide job training in computer skills. This training usually exists in those areas with a high demand for word-processing and data-processing skills.

Work Settings for THS Workers

The THS industry has long been portrayed as catering exclusively to a market for clerical employment. (By "market" we mean the particular mixes of occupations and user firm industry characteristics which have been targeted as market niches by the THS industry.) The evidence suggests that other markets, particularly the industrial and medical markets, have recently grown in importance.

Using data from the Census of Service Industries, Abraham (1988b) found that between 1972 and 1982 nonoffice temporary help employment (comprised mostly of industrial help) grew much more rapidly (13.9 percent yearly) than the 7.7 percent annual growth rate reached by office temporary help employment. Agencies specializing in nonoffice temporaries accounted for only a third of total temporary help service employment in 1972, but by 1982, comprised more than 45 percent of the total (Abraham, 1988b, p. 5). Uchitelle (1988) notes that Manpower Inc., the largest THS supplier, assigns a third of its workers to in-factory jobs. The electronics and defense industries with fluctuating orders are reportedly heavy users. Digital Equipment Corporation, the computer manufacturer,

Between 1972 and 1982 nonoffice temporary help employment grew much more rapidly than office temporary help employment.

58

reports that about 3,200 persons, about 10 percent of U.S. workers in its manufacturing division, are full-time temporary workers.[14]

As estimated by Carey and Hazelbaker,[15] the *industrial* help market accounted for approximately 30 percent of the THS industry's employment in 1984. This includes industrial workers (helpers, laborers, and materials movers) and employees in service occupations such as food and beverage preparation workers. These jobs have low-skill requirements and THS workers receive lower pay rates than regular employees in the same kinds of jobs. The major user industries are wholesale and retail trade, construction, manufacturing, and transportation, who use temps to cover work overloads. The industrial THS market may have institutionalized what used to be casual industrial labor markets (Mangum, Mayall, and Nelson, 1985). Some THS firms reportedly have replicated the traditional "shape-up" practices of casual labor in construction and agriculture. THS workers must report at the firm's office where work crews are assembled, transported to the job in company vehicles, and returned to the THS office at the end of the day (Carey and Hazelbaker, 1986).

The industrial help market accounted for approximately 30 percent of the THS industry's employment in 1984.

The office market accounted for about half of the THS employment in 1984. Almost all industries use office THS workers including clerical workers, accountants, and marketing and sales workers. But the major industry users are services, wholesale, and retail trade; manufacturing and finance; and insurance and real estate (Carey and Hazelbaker, 1986). The demand for these types of office workers is less sensitive to seasonal and cyclical changes than is the case for industrial workers and engineering and technical workers.

In 1984 the medical market accounted for 10 percent of THS employment, employing registered nurses (RNs) and licensed practical nurses (LPNs) (Carey and Hazelbaker, 1986). This market emerged in the 1970s partly in response to a national nursing shortage and to changes in Medicare reimbursements which fueled a growth in the temporary home health care market. Hospitals primarily use RNs. Nursing homes and private households use RNs and LPNs, but also have a need for nurses' aides, orderlies, and attendants.

The engineering and technical market employs professionals and accounts for only a small share of THS employment. It consists mostly of "job shops" which primarily employ engineers, designers, nonmedical technicians, and programmers. The bulk of customers are in defense-related industries such as aerospace manufacturing, electronics manufacturing, and ship building and repairing, sectors in which workload is paced by large-scale and irregular contracting. Assignments are often for a specific project and can last for relatively long periods of time.

Direct Hires and On-Call Workers

Firms also hire their own contingent workers directly without an intermediary. They may do so as a substitute for THS workers or, increasingly, in addition to temp use. Although there are no national data on direct hires, several small-scale surveys indicate that this practice has grown during the 1980s. A recent Conference Board survey reports an increased use of direct hires from 1985 to 1987 among 502 firms in manufacturing, finance and insurance, and nonfinancial services. Among these firms, direct hires were also the contingent arrangement most likely to be considered for future use.[16]

Unlike THS employment, there is no typical form for directly hiring contingent workers. Some workers belong to *on-call* pools, which are structured internal temp pools. Others are *limited-duration* (or short-term) employees, hired individually for a position often advertised as "short-term," whether or not the assignment turns out to be temporary. *On-call pools* are the most visible form of direct hiring. On-call pools were adopted by some hospitals during the 1980s to substitute for THS use. Only very recently have some large service sector employers, such as the Bank of Boston, established a formal internal temp pool for which advertising and recruitment takes place independently of the hiring of regular personnel.

A direct hire employee can face a variety of short or long-term job assignments with variable wages and employment protections. Due to this variation, there is little consensus among observers about what to call these workers. The research reported here uses the following terms: limited-duration, short-term, nonpermanent, call-ins, and on-call workers. The surveys discussed below constitute the only systematic data on the direct hiring by firms of contingent workers. The information presented relates to firm practices only—worker characteristics were unavailable.

Employer Surveys

In a May 1986 study conducted by the Bureau of National Affairs (Abraham, 1988a), human resource executives at 442 private firms were interviewed about their use of contingent workers during the year 1985, specifically: *THS workers; short-term hires* (on the company payroll for a specific period of time or for a specific project); and *on-call* workers (part of a company pool and called in on an as-needed basis). The survey results point to an across-the-board growth in all short-term employment arrangements from 1980 to 1985. Over 90 percent of the 442 firms surveyed reported using at least one of the three categories of workers during 1985, an indication of the widespread nature of these practices (see Table 6).

Abraham (1988b) estimates that if these proportions hold true for all other firms in the economy, then the total use of *all* types of contingent workers is probably over twice as large as the use of THS workers alone. Using an unofficial 1986 estimate of average THS employment (750,000 persons), Abraham estimates that the aggregate employment of *all* types of contingent workers, including THS workers, would average over 1.5 million persons for that year (Abraham, 1988b, p. 7).

The total use of all types of contingent workers is probably over twice as large as the use of THS workers alone.

TABLE 6
Growth in the Use of Temporary Workers and Outside Contractors
Bureau of National Affairs Survey

Percent of firms reporting use in 1985 compared to use in 1980, relative to regular employment

	Greater	Less	About the same	DK/no answer
THS Workers	40%	15%	40%	5%
Short-term hires	25	12	54	10
On-call workers	15	4	69	11
Administrative/business support contracts	13	6	67	14
Production subcontracting	13	6	66	16

Source: Abraham, 1988b.

A majority of users of short-term hires and slightly less than half of users of on-call workers reported that these direct hires received lower per-hour compensation than regular workers in comparable jobs (Abraham, 1988b). Table 7 presents the Bureau of National Affairs (BNA) survey results on the relative hourly costs (direct wage and benefit costs) of contingent versus regular workers. Hourly costs for THS workers were reported higher than those of regular workers while direct hires of temporary workers were less expensive.

According to Abraham (1988b), respondent firms in the survey use contingent workers to handle workload fluctuations including special projects, seasonal needs, vacancies, and as a buffer to protect the regular workforce from downturns in demand (Table 8).

The BNA survey shows industry variation in the use of contingent employment. Among manufacturing user firms, 57 percent used short-term hires, 49 percent used on-call workers, and 35 percent used THS workers, mostly in production/service jobs. Among nonmanufacturing users, 85 percent used short-term hires, 82 percent used on-call

> *A majority of users of short-term hires reported that direct hires received lower per-hour compensation than regular workers in comparable jobs.*

TABLE 7
Costs of Using Temporary Workers Compared with Costs of Using Regular Workers
Bureau of National Affairs Survey

	THS workers	Short-term hires	On-Call workers
Percent of users reporting direct costs of temporary workers versus regular employees			
Generally higher	42%	6%	11%
Generally about the same	30	33	46
Generally Lower	27	60	43
Sample size	330	273	156
Number of users	339	282	161

Source: Abraham, 1988b.

workers, and 100 percent used THS workers mostly for clerical/office positions. Finally, among health care industry users, 92 percent used on-call workers, 64 percent used short-term hires, and 33 percent used THS workers for mostly professional/technical job slots (BNA, 1986, p. 7).[17]

Another user firm survey conducted in 1981 compares the use of call-ins, limited-duration hires (LDHs, short-term hires), and Temporary Help Supply workers in 882 firms in twenty large metropolitan areas (Mangum, Mayall, and Nel-

TABLE 8
Percent of Respondents Reporting Various Reasons for Use of THS Workers, Short-term Hires, and On-call Workers
Bureau of National Affairs Survey

	THS workers	Short-term hires	On-call workers	Any of the preceding
Special projects	70%	56%	51%	77%
Seasonal needs	24	53	39	52
Provide a buffer for regular staff against downturns in demand	14	8	20	22
Any of the above	79	84	73	90
Fill vacancy until regular employee is hired	61	15	34	60
Fill in for absent regular employee	74	42	68	80
Either of the above	88	48	72	89
Identify good candidates for regular jobs	16	14	9	23
Special expertise possessed by flexible staffer	12	13	34	29
Prefer not to hire regular employees for some ongoing jobs	15	10	13	20
Other	2	10	9	11
Sample size	338	282	158	412
Total number of users	339	282	161	413

Source: Abraham, 1988a.

son, 1985). It includes six industrial sectors chosen because they have either extensive or limited use of THS workers as assessed in prior industry case studies (Mangum, Mayall, and Nelson, 1985; Mayall and Nelson, 1982). These sectors include health care, business services, finance and insurance, retail trade, transportation, and manufacturing. This survey constitutes the only source of firm-level information for the early 1980s. The results which follow are not comparable to those of the BNA survey because the sample compositions and questions differ.

The use of call-ins, limited duration hires, and THS workers increases with firm size.

Mayall and Nelson found that the use of call-ins, limited-duration hires, and THS workers increases with firm size (Table 9) with large firms making significantly greater use of LDHs and THS workers. Table 10 shows that firms with more variable product demand, as proxied by employment variability, are slightly more likely to use all three forms of contingent employment. In addition, the higher the level of fringe benefits for regular workers, the more likely firms were to use call-ins or THS workers. (This association did not hold as clearly for limited-duration hires. See Table 11.)

Table 12 shows that health care firms were more likely to use call-ins (34.0 percent) and THS workers (58.3 percent) than limited-duration hires. Conversely, firms in retail trade were more likely to use LDHs (48.5 percent) than THS workers (14.0 percent). Retail trade firms were the second

TABLE 9
Temporary Worker Usage by Size of Firm, 1981
Mangum, Mayall, and Nelson Survey

Firm size (number of employees)	Percent of Firms Using:			
	THS workers	Call-in workers	Limited-duration hires	Any of the preceding
1-41	2.7%	12.7%	36.0%	56.7%
5-19	25.7	11.4	28.3	55.7
20-49	27.1	10.5	30.1	60.2
50-99	40.5	19.0	23.8	65.5
100-249	55.6	16.5	30.9	84.5
250-299	68.9	26.7	30.0	90.0
1000+	74.7	35.2	45.6	98.9

TABLE 10
Temporary Workers Usage by Stability of Employment, 1981
Mangum, Mayall, and Nelson Survey

	Percent of Firms Using:			
Employment Variability[1]	THS workers	Call-in workers	Limited-duration hires	Any of the preceding
Numbers employed over the past 5 years:				
Increased	47.0%	18.3%	34.6%	73.6%
Decreased	41.1	22.5	27.9	72.1
Stayed the same	27.1	12.7	35.3	66.4
New firm	21.3	9.8	18.0	44.2

[1] Employment variability is used here as a proxy for demand variability.
Source: Mangum, Mayall, and Nelson, 1985.

TABLE 11
Usage of Temporary Workers by Benefit Level, 1981
Mangum, Mayall, and Nelson Survey

	Percent of Firms Using:			
Benefits[1]	THS workers	Call-in workers	Limited-duration hires	Any of the preceding
0-14%	14.6	15.6	27.3	52.2
15-19%	29.1	19.8	36.0	65.1
20-24%	35.0	11.3	34.0	69.0
25-34%	54.6	19.7	34.3	77.7
35% and over	53.0	24.5	28.5	87.8

[1] Benefits for permanent employees, as percent of total payroll.
Source: Mangum, Mayall, and Nelson, 1985.

TABLE 12
Usage of Temporary Workers by Industry, 1981
Mangum, Mayall, and Nelson Survey

	Percent of Firms Using:			
	THS workers	Call-in workers	Limited-duration hires	Any of the preceding
Health care	58.3%	34.0%	26.4%	73.6%
Retail trade	14.0	22.8	48.5	68.4
Business services	35.0	14.2	20.7	65.7
Finance, insurance	49.7	9.8	23.9	66.3
Transportation	22.5	13.4	42.5	77.5
Manufacturing	42.7	9.6	22.3	61.2
Total	37.9	16.8	32.0	69.0

Firms use different types of direct hires for distinct purposes.

heaviest user of call-ins. Finance and insurance firms were the lowest users of call-ins (9.8 percent) compared with 23.9 percent who reported using LDHs. About half the firms using LDHs also used THS workers, the highest reported multiple use of these two forms of employment (Mayall and Nelson, 1982, p. 42).

These results suggest a wide variation across industrial sectors in the type of contingent employment used and in the extent of substitution of one form of contingent employment for another. Unlike the BNA results, which report an absence of substitution, this survey points to significant variation in how firms in each sector substitute one form of contingent employment for another. Finally, limited-duration hires tend to have the longest assignments followed by THS workers, and then call-ins (Table 13). This information on length of assignment makes clear that firms use different types of direct hires for distinct purposes.

Individual Cases of Direct Hires

Some observers contend that very large employers and small firms are more likely to directly hire temporary workers than medium-sized companies (Nelson, 1988). Large employers can realize economies of scale by setting up a formal internal temp pool while small employers, to avoid the THS fee, rely on very informal practices such as intermittent call-ins.

TABLE 13
Duration of Temporary Assignments by Type, 1981
Mangum, Mayall, and Nelson Survey

	Percent of Assignments That Are:		
	THS workers	Call-in workers	Limited-duration hires
Duration in days:			
1-2	23.4%	45.7%	7.8%
3-5	33.8	22.9	15.6
6-29	33.8	24.2	26.7
30 and over	9.2	7.2	50.0
Average number of days	11.8	11.4	26.6

Source: Mangum, Mayall, and Nelson, 1985.

Partly because of its sheer size and because its personnel practices are a matter of public record, the federal government is the most well-known case of direct hiring of temporary workers. In early 1986, approximately 300,000 temporaries worked in executive offices (Nelson, 1988, p. 51). In 1985, the Office of Personnel Management (OPM) authorized federal agencies to extend "temporary limited appointments" from its original one-year limit to up to four consecutive years. In addition, the OPM raised the highest job grade for which temporaries could be hired, from GS-7 to GS-12, allowing the hiring of professional temporary employees (BNA, 1987).[18] Agencies may use limited appointments for such purposes as filling vacancies in jobs that may be contracted out or to save jobs for permanent workers whose jobs have been eliminated. Temporary hires are not required to be civil servants.

The most well-known private sector "on-call" worker pool was set up in 1981 by the national insurance firm, Travelers Corporation. This on-call pool consists of many of the company's own retirees, and is used to fill approximately 70 percent of the corporation's temporary jobs. About 10 percent of the workers in this pool are involved in job-sharing programs (two workers splitting one position), while the other 90 percent are employed on an

The federal government is the most well-known case of direct hiring of temporary workers.

on-call basis. Hourly pay for these workers is at the mid-point of the salary range for a particular job. In 1986, about 600 retirees were involved in the program, half of them former Travelers employees (BNA, 1987).

Other companies known to directly hire their temporary workers include Standard Oil of Ohio, the Grumman Corporation, Digital Corporation, ARCO, Apple Computer Inc., Intel Corporation, Hunt-Wesson and Beatrice Foods, and Hewlett-Packard. Of the 160 temporary employees working in the Philadelphia home office of CIGNA Corporation in 1985, 60 percent were hired directly by the company. Control Data Corporation has set up its own temporary agency out of Baltimore (Nine to Five, 1986, p. 13). Another well-known case is that of Motorola Inc. which, since the 1970s, has developed a hierarchy of job security for its 90,000 employees. About 30 percent of its workers, those with at least ten years seniority, are guaranteed a job. A second class, 40 percent, are regular employees who are not protected against layoffs. The remaining 30 percent hold six-month contracts that Motorola can terminate with twenty-four hours' notice (Pollock, 1986, p. 53).

Other Forms of Direct Hiring of Temporary or Contingent Workers

In addition to on-call pools and short-term hires, there are other ways in which firms have created "buffer workforces" (Gutchess, 1985). One practice relies upon *independent contractors* to perform specific tasks for finite periods of time. Independent contractors may work at home or on the company's premises. They are self-employed workers rather than wage and salary workers. However, they are *not* freelance professionals with several clients, as the term "self-employed" has implied traditionally. Rather, they work for a single company and have little of the autonomy of free-lancing with all of its risks. They are usually dependent on contract work provided by that company but may have no guarantee of a specific amount of work. Contractors are responsible for their own payments to federal insurance programs such as Social Security, Unemployment Insurance, and Workers Compensation Insurance (Christensen, 1988a).

National statistics on the self-employed do not separate out this specific category of *independent contractors* but surveys provide some indication of growth. Total nonagricultural self-employment grew from 5.2 million in 1970 to

Self-employment [including independent contract work] grew from 5.2 million in 1970 to 7.6 million in 1983.

7.6 million in 1983, a 45 percent increase (Becker, 1984).[19] In a Conference Board survey, of the 472 firms who reported using contingent workers in 1987, over 300 hired independent contractors. However, the number of these workers was rather small with 75 percent of the firms using 20 or fewer independent contractors (Conference Board, 1989, p. 9).

Another way for firms, especially manufacturers, to use contingent, or buffer, workforces has been to rely upon the contracting out of business services. How many business services sector jobs can be considered contingent or temporary remains unassessed. Using a special (twelve-month) extract from the 1983 Current Population Survey, Abraham (1988b, p. 19) reports that average wages for less skilled workers (information clerks, mail clerks and messengers, guards, and building services personnel) employed in the business services sector are from 15 to 30 percent lower than average wages for workers holding similar jobs in manufacturing and are also lower than average wages for the private sector as a whole. Using the March 1985 and March 1987 CPS, Abraham also reports that such workers are less than half as likely as similar workers in the manufacturing sector to have health insurance coverage through their employer and only 20–35 percent as likely to be covered by a pension plan (Abraham, 1988b, p. 20).

The poorer working conditions of workers in business services firms is of particular importance given the apparent increase in contracting out. About 67 percent of firms surveyed by the BNA in 1985 reported that they had contracted for administrative/business support services. Additionally, 66 percent of the firms surveyed reported some contracting out of production/service operations (subcontracting) which accounted for less than 5 percent of total production (see Table 6). Results from a 1986 Bureau of Labor Statistics special survey of business establishments in four manufacturing industries that had increased output and decreased employment from 1969 to 1984 found that a majority of establishments did contract with another firm for some services such as payroll, data processing, trucking, and janitorial services.[20] One-fifth of the establishments used THS workers, leased employees, or contract workers. (Often, the contract workers were former employees working on a special project.) The survey also found that large establishments, with 250 or more workers, were more likely to use nonpayroll workers than small or medium-

Another way for firms, especially manufacturers, to use contingent, or buffer workforces has been to rely upon the contracting out of business services.

69

sized firms (Norwood, 1988, pp. 3–4). Norwood (1988) notes that this practice is in sharp contrast to the more common forms of subcontracting (of production activities per se) which are most prevalent among small establishments with less than fifty workers. Manufacturing firms which are often restricted by union contract in hiring temporary and part-time workers are more apt to contract out peripheral activities (BNA, 1987).

Another way for firms to hire buffer workers has been through *two-tier contracts with union organizations.*[21] In these cases, new hires are paid a lower hourly rate, may not be eligible for some pension benefits, and may have less protection from layoffs than the regular workers. These agreements, often forced upon union locals in weak bargaining positions, have proved difficult to maintain over time because of their divisive nature and their effects on employee morale (*New York Times,* 1987; *Business Week,* 1987).

Explanation for the Growth of Temporary Employment

Two major arguments have been put forth to account for the rapid growth of temporary work arrangements during the 1980s. Some argue that the growth is "supply-led," determined by workers' needs for "nonstandard" work arrangements. Others contend that the growth is "demand-led," determined by the needs of individual firms for labor flexibility.

Due to the dearth of information on temporary workers, research has not yet led to a consensus on how firms use these workers, their patterns of use, and whether or not workers want these jobs. In particular, insufficient data constrain our ability to assess the use of direct hires. Nevertheless, we can use recent analyses of changes in employment systems to gain an understanding of the context in which contingent employment has grown. There is also new research which has yielded consistent results on the sources of growth in the THS industry. These results suggest that it is changes in firms' demands for labor rather than workers' preferences which have spawned the industry's growth. If these results also hold for explaining the growth of direct hires, we will be able to more strongly assert that the expansion of contingent employment

It is changes in firms' demands for labor rather than workers' preferences which have spawned the industry's growth.

reflects structural changes in the demand of labor in the U.S. economy.

A Supply-Led Growth

There is no question that both the composition and the preferences of the workforce changed during the 1970s and 1980s. What is at issue is the *extent* to which these two tendencies have contributed to the growth of temporary employment.

"Supply-led growth" arguments assert that the expansion in temporary employment is driven by changing demographics in the labor force. Over the past twenty-five years, the workforce has come to include increasing numbers of women with preschool and school-age children, as well as teenagers and retirees. These worker groups hold work and career attitudes that are significantly different from those of prime-age, married males who have traditionally constituted the core of the U.S. workforce. Women workers with children may want shorter work weeks, and teenagers and retirees may want intermittent work. Neither of these groups may think of staying with the same employer for extended periods of time.

Worker preferences have changed as well. An increasing number of workers, including prime-age working males, seek variety and flexibility in their work lives and thus give less value to the benefits associated with long-term employment such as promotion, training, and pensions. In this view, contingent employment has expanded to meet the needs of the contemporary workforce. In the case of temp industry employment, the "supply-led growth" argument further contends that there has been a good match between worker needs and specific labor supply bottlenecks.

Recent research on causes underlying growth trends in THS employment finds little evidence to support the labor supply thesis. Lapidus (1989) has explored reasons behind the concentration of women workers in the industry by comparing the characteristics of female THS workers in a special supplement to the May 1985 Current Population Survey with those of a random sample of all non-THS female workers from the same survey. There are few, if any, statistically significant differences between female THS employees and the general female labor force in terms of marital status, number and age of children, educational level, and average hourly wages ($5.96 per hour for THS workers and $5.92 per hour for all women). However,

Recent research on causes underlying growth trends in THS employment finds little evidence to support the labor supply thesis.

71

female THS workers tend to be younger on average (34.24 years), than their counterparts in the labor force (37.32 years). Lapidus also tested the impact of family responsibilities on the likelihood of being a THS employee.[22] Her results do not support the hypothesis that the THS industry attracts women who are more likely to have family responsibilities. In fact, results suggest that women's family responsibilities constrain their job options, whether in THS or other employment, and/or that the industry's growth is demand-led (Lapidus, 1989).

As is the case with female THS workers, male THS workers are younger than other male workers (mean age of 32 years vs. 39). However, male temps have lower levels of educational attainment, and much lower wage levels (mean of $5.39 an hour vs. $10.02 an hour) than do other male workers. Lapidus also finds that married men are much less likely to work in temporary employment than unmarried men.[23]

Golden and Appelbaum (1990) also present results which show that from 1982 to 1987,[24] all other things being equal, an influx of women, youth, or older workers in the workforce has not generated a growth in THS jobs (Golden and Appelbaum, 1990, p. 26). The authors conclude that if women are concentrated in THS employment it is because THS jobs are similar to jobs women can obtain in the economy at large and not because temporary employment better meets the flexibility needs of married women workers (Golden and Appelbaum, 1990, p. 28). They concur with Lapidus that the concentration of women in the THS industry reflects the increasing availability of temp jobs and their similarity to "female jobs" in the economy. To date, there has been no systematic research on whether or not growth in the use of direct hires is tied to changes in workforce composition and worker preferences. Such research will need to distinguish among the varieties of direct-hires employment including short-term hires and on-call pools.

A Demand-Led Growth

If changes in labor force composition are not sufficient to explain the accelerated growth of contingent employment during the 1980s, then we must look to explanations which relate this phenomenon to structural changes in employer practices.

Contingent employment arrangements, including temporary employment, employee leasing, and contracting-out,

> *Lapidus' results do not support the hypothesis that the THS industry attracts women who are more likely to have family responsibilities.*

appear to be part of a broader strategy to cut labor costs and improve firm competition.[25] In the late 1970s and 1980s, new economic conditions increased the variability and uncertainty in product demand, expanded and internationalized the scope of markets, and decreased firm market shares. These new features of competition have pressured firms to cut labor costs; to achieve greater flexibility in the quantity and skills of their workforce; and, according to some, to alter firm boundaries by shifting the costs and risks of production onto subcontractors and contingent workers.[26]

In the view of several labor market analysts, the growth of contingent employment is evidence that employment practices in large firms are changing. Training ladders have been compressed, firm-specific training has become less important, and external recruitment for middle-level positions has increased (facilitated by growth of higher education degrees). As a result, we have witnessed the development of contingent employment particularly, but not exclusively, at the bottom of occupational structures where skills are easily acquired and at the top where skills are portable across firms (see Appelbaum, 1987; Christopherson, 1986; Noyelle, 1987).

Osterman (1987, 1988) concurs with this view and contends that similar work can be performed in very different hiring, training, promotion, and turnover patterns. Firms have choices regarding these patterns.[27] And, over time, firms can alter their internal systems of employment. Within firms, labor market practices tend to be organized around one of two models: the industrial model or the salaried model. These major systems are then combined with other forms of employment: a secondary subsystem (e.g., low-skill clerical employment), where we find most temporary employment, also termed "secondary arrangements," and a craft subsystem of workers who are higher skilled but still highly mobile across firms (e.g., computer programming). Each employment model consists of rules and procedures which govern job definition and classification, workforce deployment, job security, and wage setting.

According to Osterman, the growth of "secondary arrangements" is evidence that the industrial and the salaried models are under pressure. The industrial model, prevalent in unionized blue-collar employment, relies on strict job classifications, and nonpersonalistic rules and procedures (e.g., seniority) as the key to job security and worker

Contingent employment arrangements appear to be part of a broader strategy to cut labor costs and improve firm competition.

cooperation. This model is under pressure from the implementation of new technologies which mandate broader job definitions and more flexibility in job assignment. It is also under pressure from competitive changes and the need, in some industries, to downscale production. The salaried model, prevalent in salaried white-collar employment (and in innovative blue-collar employment settings) entails broad job definitions and greater flexibility in assignment. The key to its stability is the implicit promise of employment security.[28] This system is under pressure and risks being undermined by the threat of layoffs and workforce contraction. In this context, secondary arrangements have expanded both as stop-gap measures and as critical features of changing employment. Osterman contends that there is a risk that secondary arrangements will become an entrenched practice in large internal labor markets, working against firm stability and efficiency.

Golden and Appelbaum (1990) agree that firms' primary purpose in increasing their use of contingent employment during the 1980s was to cut labor costs, but observe that the particular appeal of contingent employment for firms is also in allowing them to restore management prerogatives in controlling work schedules, assignments, and other aspects of the production process. They argue that contingent employment is only one way to achieve labor-cost reductions to meet the requirements of increased price competition; other options include improvements in labor productivity and the cross-training of workers. However, contingent employment is particularly appealing because it can serve both as a cost-cutting tool and as a disciplinary tool. Its use has increased as union power has waned in many workplaces, facilitated by decreasing unionization rates and a hostile legal climate for unionization drives (Golden and Appelbaum, 1990, p. 8).

In their study of temp (THS) industry employment trends from 1982 to 1987, Golden and Appelbaum present evidence both on the role of unionization and the role of demand-side variables in the accelerated growth of the industry. They find that a decline in relative union bargaining power has increased the ability of employers to expand their temp workforces.[29] They also report that several demand-side variables have a significant influence on the growth of temp employment:

1. a rise in the level of demand for output above its long-term trend (however, an increase in last year's output

> *A decline in relative union bargaining power has increased the ability of employers to expand their temp workforces.*

could lead employers to reduce their current demand for temp workers in favor of building their permanent workforces);

2. the intensification of international cost competition;
3. the growth of fixed, nonwage, labor costs relative to wage costs;
4. the availability of paid time off for the regular workforce;
5. the need to adjust the workweek of the regular workforce; and
6. the expansion in skill requirements within a firm requiring the use of temps until a permanent worker is hired (Golden and Appelbaum, 1990, p. 25).

The research outlined above suggests that changes in firm demand for labor rather than changes in workers' preferences have driven the rapid growth of contingent employment during the 1980s. Reducing labor costs, adapting to variability in demand, and increasing flexibility in labor inputs are goals which have motivated much of the increase in firm demand for THS employment, and, most likely, for other forms of contingent employment. If results on the role of demand-side variables persist, further research will be needed to examine industry-by-industry the circumstances under which contingent work arrangements emerge and the conditions which govern their particular form.

By entering the labor market through those jobs, women may see their options for future advancement limited.

Causes for Worry?

The expansion of contingent employment poses risks to workers and to the firms who use temporary employees.

The Risks to the Workforce

With contingent employment, workers encounter the possibility of reduced protection from labor and social legislation. Contingent employment, on its face, appears to suit women workers with a tenuous attachment to the labor market by permitting part-year, part-time, and intermittent work. In fact, contingent jobs are often the mechanism by which women enter, or reenter, the workforce. As ports of entry, however, these jobs often are not connected to the rest of the employment structure within a firm. Thus, by entering the labor market through those jobs, women may see their options for future advancement limited.

Black male workers often find their possibilities for future career opportunities also limited by contingent employment. The overrepresentation of black men in the temp (THS) industry may reflect the unavailability of regular employment and be their only hope against unemployment. For black males, contingent employment opportunities mirror the types of low-wage jobs many hold in the economy at large.

Thus, contingent employment may weaken the promise and implementation of equal employment opportunity policies which have been built around the monitoring of hiring, pay, and promotion practices for regular workers. For instance, a study conducted by the National Planning Association reports that out of fifty American companies using contingent employment, only one corporation had "even bothered to look" at its equal employment opportunity implications (Hartmann and Lapidus, 1989, p. 17).

The Risks to Firms

For firms, the use of contingent employment may be costlier than first appears because of its long-term consequences in unrealized potential productivity gains. Workers hired on contingent arrangements do not acquire firm-specific skills and do not develop an allegiance to their place of employment. In fact, there is little incentive for firms to train these workers and to make the most productive use of new technologies. Appelbaum (1987) argues that in order to maximize the potential productivity increases from new computer technologies and new forms of organizing production, firms need a skilled and responsible workforce. Yet, by using contingent employment, they may ultimately jeopardize this potential in their need to cut short-term labor costs.

The Current State of Policy

The Need for Improved Data Collection

Perhaps the most compelling policy concern regarding temporary employment is the need for a systematic and sustained data series on the THS industry and its workers and, more importantly, on direct hires. What our survey of existing information sources has made very clear is that we know little about the extent of these short-term arrange-

> *The overrepresentation of black men in the temp industry may reflect the unavailability of regular employment and may be their only hope against unemployment.*

ments and the characteristics of the workers and firms involved.

Survey information is needed on the extent of worker choice involved in short-term employment. Such surveys should yield data on the share of short-term workers seeking permanent employment, including their perceptions of the duration of the transition from contingent to regular employment. Needed also is information on the career patterns, job security, and hours variability of cohorts of these workers.[30] Surveys should explore what features of short-term employment workers like and dislike. Research should also document the actual number of contingent workers who receive health and retirement benefits, including the source and type of these protections. Finally, research should investigate how the unemployment insurance system affects THS workers. For instance, are spells of assignments for some categories of workers so short that they rarely qualify for unemployment insurance benefits?

Existing Policy and Regulation

Federal Protection for THS Workers. The extent of federal protection for short-term and temporary workers depends greatly on the extent of their ties to a particular employer. As Mayall and Nelson (1982) pointed out, THS agencies are not regulated at the federal level. And, unlike personnel employment agencies (placement services), THS agencies are also not regulated at the state level. The THS agency has responsibility for carrying out the provisions of the Fair Labor Standards Act, the Equal Employment Opportunity Act, and the Occupational Health and Safety Act. But there is some ambiguity as to who has the legal responsibility for worker protection in cases of payrolling or "try before you hire" agreements between the THS and the user firm.

The ambiguity is an issue of great concern in the case of the enforcement of Occupational Health and Safety regulation, particularly in manufacturing, construction, and health care. "The implicit sharing of responsibility involved when an employee of one firm works at the site of another is legally recognized by the designation of the firms as joint employers under state and federal statute" (Mayall and Nelson, 1982, p. 124). Unfortunately, this double employment relationship allows some workers in hazardous industries to "slip through the cracks" when the two employers evade responsibility.[31]

Survey information is needed on the extent of worker choice involved in short-term employment.

Even if there is a strong commitment to enforcement on the part of an individual THS agency, Mayall and Nelson point out, it is difficult for it to be fully aware of all safety factors involved in manufacturing processes and to take precautions to ensure worker safety (1982, p. 52).

Federal protection for direct hire temporaries should not, in principle, be any different from that available to the permanent workforce, assuming they work in the same worksite under the same employment conditions. It is more likely to be substantially different in cases in which entire departments are staffed by direct hires on short assignments.[32]

Unemployment Insurance (UI) Protections. In qualifying for UI benefits, temporary workers encounter difficulties similar to part-time workers. Minimum earnings requirements specified by state laws (usually over a six-month period) disqualify large numbers of both part-time and short-term workers. (Unfortunately we do not have accurate figures on the share of workers who are ineligible.) Additionally, the unemployment insurance system contains a built-in incentive for THS agencies to prevent workers from qualifying for UI benefits. Employer contributions to the UI system are based on an unemployment experience rating which, given the nature of temporary employment, is inherently high in most THS companies. To keep its experience rating in check, a THS company can offer a one-day assignment to an individual worker when the worker is about to qualify for unemployment registration, usually at the end of the first week of full-time unemployment.[33]

Finally, UI regulations in all but six states deny unemployment benefits to any worker who limits his or her eligibility to part-time work (Pierce cited in Nine to Five, 1986). These restrictions hurt all part-time THS workers.

Federal Regulation and Pensions. The area in which federal law has the greatest impact upon contingent employment is that of pension regulation. The Employee Retirement Income Security Act (ERISA) requires companies with pension plans to extend pension benefits to employees who work 1,000 hours or more a year (about twenty hours per week). To circumvent the law, employers can preclude coverage of direct hires (or reduce the amount of their pensions) by keeping yearly total hours below this threshold. For example, the Travelers Insurance Company, which has a well-publicized on-call pool of retirees, keeps

> The unemployment insurance system contains a built-in incentive for THS agencies to prevent workers from qualifying for UI benefits.

the work hours of these workers at or below 960 hours per year to prevent them from accruing additional pension credits that would increase their pension income (Nine to Five, 1986, p. 23).

Pension regulation for short-term hires leased from outside agencies is more complicated.[34] The Tax Equity and Fiscal Responsibility Act of 1982 requires that the THS agency or leasing company provide pension benefits to those employees who work for a user firm providing a pension plan and who have completed twelve months of substantially full-time service of 1,500 hours yearly, almost twenty-nine hours per week (Fromstein, 1988, p. 99). For THS workers, it is possible to keep continuous assignments with a single employer below this threshold. For leased employees, a 1986 modification to the Tax Equity Fiscal Responsibility Act (TEFRA) mandates that companies in which 20 percent of the workforce are leased cover those workers in its pension plan.[35] In practice, user firms avoid this threshold by keeping temps on assignments ranging between 600 to 1,000 hours, as reported by Manpower Inc., a major THS firm. Frequently, the temp worker is reassigned to a different client firm for the balance of the working year.[36]

Labor Law. Collective bargaining on behalf of temporary workers or direct hires is difficult to achieve under current labor law. The National Labor Relations Board has based the inclusion of short-term hires in the bargaining unit using a criterion of "community of interests" between the permanent and temporary workforces. The Board has, however, defined this community of interest on a case-by-case basis (Bronfenbrenner, 1988b, p. 10).

The exclusion of temporary workers from collective bargaining prevents unions from extending benefits, such as group health insurance, to this workforce. In addition, this exclusion makes it difficult for unions to secure the right of contingent workers to move from a temporary status to a permanent status.

Including direct hires into the bargaining unit would require unions to manage two goals that at times might seem contradictory. One objective is to protect these workers; the other is to prevent the wholesale conversion of permanent full-time jobs into temporary work. In both cases, union involvement would ensure that workers' interests are represented in how employment relationships are structured within the firm.

The exclusion of temporary workers from collective bargaining prevents unions from extending benefits, such as group health insurance, to this workforce.

Future Implications for Employment Policy

Antidiscrimination Policy

A number of significant achievements toward workforce equity have been advanced under the aegis of antidiscrimination policy. However, when personnel policies separate direct hires from regular workers, contingent workers may be unable to claim comparable terms of employment (such as wage parity), even though they share the same work functions (Christopherson, 1988, p. 21).

Strategies for implementing pay equity, such as job evaluation studies, look for discrimination within existing pay scales of the regular workforce. The fact that temp workers and direct hires are not on the same pay scale as regular workers weakens the effects of this strategy. Equal Employment Opportunity monitoring by firms and by government agencies has thus far not been modified to include contingent workers.

Changing our Conceptions of the Provision of Social Benefits

Temporary work arrangements are changing the terms and conditions of employment for large groups of workers. As significant numbers of employees work under temporary arrangements, whether by choice or for lack of better options, we need to rethink the U.S. system for the provision of social benefits. Until now, manager and worker organizations have viewed the employment relationship as the primary determinant of social welfare. However, for those workers for whom continuous attachment to a single employer is no longer the preferred choice or a realistic possibility, we may need to develop policies that transcend the employer-employee relationship. In the current era, contingent workers must carry the financial burden of their own social insurance needs. We may need to rethink benefits such as health insurance and pensions as social entitlements or rights of citizenship rather than as job-related privileges. In a history of the development of personnel practices in large firms, Sanford Jacoby (1987) argued that in the United States more than in other industrialized countries, the "social protection" tradition has become embodied in workplace benefits and personnel policies. The

In the current era, contingent workers must carry the financial burden of their own social insurance needs.

expansion of contingent employment suggests that this tradition is out of date.

Making Flexible Arrangements Work for the Workforce

There is a growing interest among workers for more flexible work arrangements. The issue for policymakers and for trade unionists is not to preclude workers from pursuing alternative work schedules but to ensure that workers do not lose key social benefits as a result.

To understand the varying needs of individual workers, we need to redefine the notion of choice. Choosing temporary employment may mean something entirely different to the freelance engineer or computer programmer than it does to the day-laborer on a construction site, or the part-time registered nurse. The fact that some workers prefer more flexible work arrangements should not blind us to the fact that contingent employment, as presently constructed, represents poor employment choices.

The challenge for policymakers and unions is to expand hard-won social benefits and employment rights—which are currently tied to traditional forms of employment—to cover workers in new employment arrangements. Strategies may include making social benefits portable, or offering workers a menu of diverse benefits from which to choose. Any solution will have to ensure that the costs of these benefits not be borne solely by individual workers, nor by individual taxation, but be shared equally with employers.

The case of health benefits coverage illustrates the limits of choices currently available. In testimony before Congress, the head of Manpower Inc. argued that only 35 percent (20,000) of employees that are eligible for the company's health plan take that coverage (amounting to about 8 percent of the company's total workforce), because a majority of these workers have coverage from another source (Fromstein, 1988, p. 111). However, only 22.8 percent (about 57,000 out of 250,000) of Manpower's workers meet the company's eligibility requirements. Thus, we don't know what the options for health care coverage really are for the majority of these workers. Additionally, on the THS-provided plan, a worker is likely to lose coverage if she or he is out of work due to illness for a month or more. To maintain coverage, he or she would have to have worked

The fact that some workers prefer more flexible work arrangements should not blind us to the fact that contingent employment, as presently constructed, represents poor employment choices.

300 hours in the previous two months or 34–35 hours per week and have maintained coverage by paying the full insurance premium while sick and not working.

Even less is known about the health care insurance choices of direct hires whose treatment varies from employer to employer. It is quite likely that company policy on health care coverage for these workers overlaps with its treatment of part-time workers in those cases where direct hires work part-time schedules.

Some advocates frame the issue of benefits for temporary workers (and for part-time workers) in terms of employment discrimination. Namely, workers with work schedules differing from those of permanent workers should not be discriminated against by employer policies and social legislation which favor full-time, full-year workers. The Part-Time and Temporary Workers Protection Act, introduced in the last two Congresses by Representative Patricia Schroeder, would mandate pro-rated health and pension benefits for these workers.

Our survey of existing evidence points out the striking need for systematic data collection on temporary workers.

Conclusion

Contingent employment takes varied forms. In this chapter we have examined the growth during the 1980s of employment in the Temporary Help Supply (THS) industry and the increase of contingent workers hired directly by firms.

Our survey of existing evidence points out the striking need for systematic data collection on temporary workers, in particular, direct hires. By all accounts, the number of direct hires far surpasses the size of employment in the THS industry. Yet we know little about the aggregate number and the characteristics of these workers.

Current data on workers in the THS industry suggest the risk of this employment. Women workers and black workers are overrepresented in the industry. Most of these workers forgo access to medical and retirement benefits. Many may become stranded in jobs which, in many instances, provide lower pay, fewer benefits, and less opportunity for on-the-job training than regular employment.

Research on the growth of the Temporary Help Supply industry during the 1980s lends little credence to the notion that the growth of contingent employment is due to changes in worker preference and workforce composition, namely the influx of mothers, teenagers, and retirees in the workplace. What underlies the growth of contingent employment in the 1980s is a more fundamental change in how firms manage their workforces. Reducing labor costs, adapting to variability in demand, and increasing flexibility in labor inputs are goals which have motivated much of the increase in firm demand for THS workers and, most likely, other forms of contingent employment.

Research is needed that examines the extent of choice in contingent work arrangements. For black workers in particular, employment in the THS industry may only be a stop-gap solution to avoid unemployment and not a way to meet special career and scheduling needs.

The sustained presence of contingent employment in many workplaces also entails risks to employers. Contingent workers acquire few firm-specific skills and firms have little incentive to train them. Consequently, firms may end up with a workforce incapable of realizing the full productivity benefits of the diffusion of microcomputer-based technologies in the workplace.

Finally, the existing system of federal and state protections for the workforce is based on the notion that employment should be full-time, year-round, and with a single employer. The proliferation of contingent arrangements in the workplace has occurred in the absence of clear government regulation concerning enforcement of equal employment opportunity laws, the Occupational Safety and Health Act, and collective bargaining. Thus, we are faced with the broader social question of who should provide employment protections for contingent workers—workers, employers, or government?

What underlies the growth of contingent employment in the 1980s is a more fundamental change in how firms manage their workforces.

Endnotes

1   The term contingent employment includes a set of jobs in one industry as well as arrangements which can cover jobs in any industry. Researchers often include in contingent employment other forms of employment such as: contracting-out of peripheral activities, employee leasing, self-employment, and part-time employment. Polivka and Nardone (1989) developed a working definition of contingent employment as "any job in which an individual does not have an explicit or implicit contract for long-term employment or one in which the minimum hours worked can vary in a non-systematic manner" (Polivka and Nardone, 1989, p. 11). The authors take issue with the notion that lack of access to benefits is a key indicator of contingent employment. For temp industry workers and for direct hires, however, the lack of access to benefits is a key aspect of conditions of employment and a key labor cost saving for firms.

2   See Gannon (1984) for reports that many temp workers seek a full-time position. Useful evidence also comes from other countries. See Cohen and White (1989) for a report that, in Canada, 41 percent of THS workers wanted full-time jobs but were unable to find them.

3   Current Employment Statistics cited in Hartmann and Lapidus (1989), p. 3.

4   National Association of Temporary Services estimate based on data reported by membership and cited in Hartmann and Lapidus (1989), p. 3.

5   This section on the THS industry relies heavily on Carey and Hazelbaker (1986). The THS industry is often taken to represent most forms of temporary employment or of personnel services but other industries provide personnel to user firms as well. They include: janitorial services (DOL Standard Industry Code SIC 7349), guard services (SIC 7393), and managerial services (SIC 7392). However, these other industries provide a specific service, the worker is supervised by the service-supplying firm and it is unclear what proportion of these jobs are temporary (Carey and Hazelbaker, 1986). Employee leasing firms (SIC 7369) is another form of personnel supply which may or may not entail temporary employment duration.

6   Mangum, Mayall, and Nelson (1985) draw a distinction between THS payrolling which entails taking over entire departments and THS assignments which are the more traditional practice of the industry.

7   According to the Bureau of Labor Statistics, 43.3 percent of the employment growth in producer services was due to higher levels of gross national product, and only 1.7 percent of the employment growth was due to changes in final demand (Belous, 1989b, p. 36).

8   This section relies heavily on Plewes (1988) and Howe (1986b).

9   There is no trend information on the workforce in THS assignments. Trend information on employment *level,* payroll, and number of establishments in the indus-

try is provided by the Current Employment Statistics from an establishment survey. A small share of these employment levels consists of jobs held by the permanent staff of agencies.

[10] The least skilled subgroup of that occupation—handlers, equipment cleaners, helpers, and laborers—accounted for 11.2 percent of black male employment and for 5.6 percent of white male employment. Data are household data, not seasonally adjusted (U.S. Department of Labor, Bureau of Labor Statistics, *Employment and Earnings,* June 1985, Table A23, p. 47).

[11] The survey conducted by the Bureau of Labor Statistics covered more than 600,000 workers in THS establishments with fifty workers or more, in all states except Alaska and Hawaii. The survey covers both "temp" and permanent staff, but results reported here only cover temps. Because of the survey design, the estimate of employment in the industry that this survey provides does not match that from the Current Employment Survey series, which is reported earlier in the report. This entire section relies on Williams (1989).

[12] Excludes premium pay for overtime and for work on weekends, holidays, and late shifts. Where applicable, incentive payments and cost-of-living increases were included as part of regular pay but performance bonuses and lump-sum payments were excluded (Williams, 1989, p. 6).

[13] The following section relies on Williams (1989).

[14] Russel Johnson, D.E.C. manager of strategic employment, cited in Uchitelle (1988).

[15] The authors use a 1984 BLS industry-occupation matrix to develop a typology of markets. See Carey and Hazelbaker (1986).

[16] The survey asked firms to report on their practices in 1987 as compared to the period 1985–86. The survey sample included 169 manufacturing firms (median workforce size of 6,500), 179 finance and insurance firms (median workforce of 3,500), and 154 nonfinancial services (median workforce of 1,400) (The Conference Board, 1989).

[17] The sample was weighted heavily toward firms in manufacturing, finance, insurance and real estate, and health care. The trade and services sectors were underrepresented. Also, small employers were not well represented in the study.

[18] Additionally, the federal government employs seasonal employees who work recurring periods of less than twelve months per year but are eligible to obtain health and life insurance benefits throughout the year. On-call employees serve when needed and have an expected cumulative service period of a minimum of six months per year. They are covered by the civil service retirement system and are eligible for health and life insurance coverage throughout the year if they pay their premium share. Intermittent employees are "without a regularly scheduled tour of duty," and are not eligible for health benefits or life insurance coverage.

[19] For a closer estimate of homeworkers in particular, the Small Business Administration has reported that women-operated sole proprietorships—a tax status often claimed by independent contractors—grew at an annual rate of 6.9 percent from 1977 to 1982 as compared to an overall rate of growth of nonfarm proprietorships of 3.7 percent (see Christensen, 1988c).

[20] Industries covered included industrial chemicals, shipbuilding, and wood household furniture.

[21] In 1985, postal workers had 720,000 workers covered by two-tier contracts; food and commercial workers had 133,000; teamsters had 100,000; machinists had 75,000; pilots' and flight attendants' unions had 35,000; and United Auto Workers had 30,000. See Bureau of National Affairs data cited in *Business Week* (1985, pp. 70–71). Numbers might have changed since with contract renewals.

[22] A logit analysis run on THS women workers and a sample of women in the labor force had a dependent variable of zero or one to indicate employment in the THS industry. Independent variables were age, marital status, education, and age of children. An "earners" variable (one if other earners present, zero otherwise) was added to capture the possible effects of women choosing THS employment because they relied on the job-related benefits received by other family members (Lapidus, 1989).

[23] The logit analysis includes the following independent variables: age, marital status, education, and number of children for a sample of male THS employees and other adult men in the labor force (Lapidus, 1989).

[24] Golden and Appelbaum develop a simple two-sector model of the labor market with a permanent employment and a temporary employment sector. The authors estimate this model using a monthly data series on THS industry employment from 1982 to 1987 done by the Bureau of Labor Statistics Survey of Establishments. Forces hypothesized to explain the level of THS employment in the literature enter into the specifications of the labor demand and labor supply functions. Labor supply and labor demand in the temp sector are functions of the ratio of temp to permanent wages (proxied by the ratio of average hourly earnings in the THS industry to earnings of production workers in manufacturing where regular, full-time employment is the norm). The reduced form equation of the determinants of the level of temp employment provides an analysis of forces influencing the growth of temp jobs. In this model, the supply of labor in the temp labor market sector may expand (contract) as slack (tight) employment conditions develop in the permanent job sector. An increase in the share of part-time employment that is involuntary is interpreted as a proxy for a decrease in the share of permanent employment because there is no direct proxy for permanent employment available.

[25] Employee leasing, although a form of contingent employment, is not covered in this report.

[26] Belous (1989b, p. 96) argues that the "New Deal" model of human resource man-

agement which sheltered workers in internal labor markets from product market forces is being replaced by the "contingent" model in which compensation levels and work rules are impacted by international economic forces and in which contingent workers play a central role in the flexible system of employment.

[27] In this view, firms have to achieve objectives of cost minimization, predictability, and flexibility under competitive and cost constraints as well as constraints generated by labor force characteristics, labor market institutions, and social organization.

[28] The implicit promise is that layoffs will either not occur or that the firm will make every reasonable effort to avoid them.

[29] As an index of relative bargaining power, the authors use union density in the overall labor force interacted with the average wage adjustment in collective bargaining contracts. The variable estimates the extent of union leverage to achieve favorable terms of employment in contracts, or alternatively, union acquiescence to management's contingent employment strategy or anti-union sentiment (Golden and Appelbaum, 1990, p. 20).

[30] See Polivka and Nardone (1989) for suggestions for a federal survey.

[31] Mayall and Nelson (1982) discuss cases of serious industrial accidents in the chemical industry. In one case, both the THS and the worksite firm received citations; in another, only the worksite firm did (p. 124).

[32] Also, because the federal government does not regulate terms and conditions of employment, there is no over-arching national legislation mandating that, in non-union settings, provisions of personnel policy available to the permanent workforce be extended to direct hires.

[33] Some temp agencies' executives interviewed by the author in the early 1980s mentioned that this practice exists in the industry.

[34] 350 employee-leasing firms employ slightly less than 200,000 persons. Leased employees work for the client firm as regular employees would. The leasing firm is the direct employer; it administers payroll, benefits, and pension plans. Leasing is used by small firms that only keep corporate officers as employees and thus avoid extending the generous pension arrangements of these officers to the rest of their workforce (Day, 1988).

[35] In the 1982 TEFRA version, the "safe harbor leasing" clause provided that client firms did not need to extend their pension plan to leased employees as long as the leasing firm provided employees with a money purchase pension to which the leasing firm contribution should be no less than 7.5 percent of employee compensation (Day, 1988, pp. 60–62).

[36] In 1988, Manpower, Inc. reported that less than 2 percent of its temp workforce was assigned to a single customer for 1,500 yearly hours or more (Fromstein, 1988, p. 99).

New Policies for the Part-Time and Contingent Workforce

Virginia L. duRivage

Introduction

Full-time permanent employment is fast becoming an anachronism in today's changing economy. Since 1973 the rate of nontraditional employment has grown faster than the rate of full-time work. By 1988, nearly twenty-seven million workers, or 23 percent of U.S. workers, were employed outside the permanent full-time labor force (Mishel and Frankel, 1991). This workforce represents a growing category of diverse work arrangements including part-time and temporary work as well as low-wage self-employment.

The expansion of contingent employment is evidence of a fundamental transformation of the arrangement of work in the advanced economies. These changes are driven, in part, by business' need for flexibility in a competitive world market. At the same time, a growing number of workers welcome part-time and temporary employment as a strategy for combining paid work and family responsibilities. Yet, for too many workers in the United States, this flexibility breeds social and economic insecurity. Many part-time and temporary jobs fail to provide guaranteed employment, fringe benefits, a living wage, any accommodation of family responsibilities, or opportunities for union representation. In some cases, the shift toward more "flexible" forms of work relieves employers of federal obligations under such programs as the Occupational Safety and Health Administration (OSHA), the Employment Retirement Income Secu-

By 1988, nearly twenty-seven million workers, or 23 percent of U.S. workers, were employed outside the permanent full-time labor force.

rity Act (ERISA), unemployment compensation, and affirmative action.

The expansion of contingent work schedules suggests that employer-employee relations have entered a new era in which the responsibilities for health care insurance, an adequate wage, and indeed, even job creation, have been shifted to individual workers and their families. Many of these workers are forced into contingent jobs by the economy's failure to generate adequate full-time employment and by the lack of a coherent public and private policy response to the needs of working families. The continued growth of part-time and temporary employment threatens to reduce the economic security of all workers and to weaken workforce productivity and efficiency.

Labor analysts and policy experts have examined different aspects of the issue, but to date, we lack a clear policy framework for dealing effectively with the contingent work problem. This paper is an effort to clarify the major economic and social issues inherent in contingent work and to formulate a set of public and private policy proposals geared toward moving contingent workers into the mainstream of job opportunity and federal protection.

Public and private employment policies in the United States are designed for full-time workers with permanent attachments to the labor force. The challenge for policymakers and for private employers is to revamp employment policy to reflect the changing profile of the American workforce. Many of the policies suggested in this paper may, in fact, appear intrusive to business, but are necessary when employers are inclined to evade their responsibilities to workers. A preferred strategy is to broaden our notions of social insurance—health care, pensions, and income security—as a right extended to all as a matter of citizenship or residence rather than a privilege conditioned by one's work status or employment relationship. There is indeed variation among Western European welfare states, but to a large extent, it is these basic social provisions, extended as a right of citizenship, rather than a privilege of employment, which have cushioned the impact of economic restructuring on workers overseas. To a similar degree, policies implemented at the national level in this country, particularly universal health insurance, pension portability, wage equity, and new forms of worker representation, can act as a buffer against economic change and ensure that "flexibility" in the marketplace benefits workers as well as employers.

> **Public and private employment policies in the United States are designed for full-time workers with permanent attachments to the labor force.**

To improve the employment and economic security of part-time and contingent workers, Congress should:

- guarantee hourly wage parity between part-time and full-time workers performing the same job;
- restore the minimum wage to its original standard of 50 percent of the median hourly wage;
- standardize eligibility requirements under state unemployment compensation systems;
- adopt pension portability measures which allow workers to carry pension credits with them to their next job; and
- replace the current employer-based system of health care insurance with a universal scheme that incorporates equal access and cost containment and is funded through tax revenues.

Lower hourly pay rates increase the economic vulnerability of marginal workers and compromise the security of other workers.

Contingent Work and the Problem of Pay

Employers often utilize part-time, temporary, and subcontracted employment as a strategy to reduce overall labor costs. Lower hourly pay rates, however, increase the economic vulnerability of marginal workers and compromise the security of other workers. Inadequate minimum wage laws and unfair tax policies exacerbate their economic situation.

Low Wages and Economic Vulnerability. Part-time workers earn about 60 percent of the hourly wages of full-time workers, earning $4.42 per hour in 1987 compared to $7.43 for full-time workers (U.S. Department of Labor, *Employment and Earnings,* January 1988). Lower hourly earnings also characterize contingent work in the temporary help supply industry. In 1987, temporary workers employed by temporary help supply agencies such as Kelly Services or Manpower, Inc. earned an average of $6.42 an hour compared to $8.98 for all nonagricultural workers and $8.47 for all service employees (U.S. Department of Labor, 1988c). Much of the hourly wage gap between part-time and full-time workers can be attributed to the concentration of part-time workers in the lower-paid retail trade and services industries and the disproportionate numbers of women, teens, and elders in the part-time labor force. Yet Tilly (1990) reported that a part-time worker, identical to a full-time worker in industry, occupation, sex, age, and other

91

characteristics still earns an average of 10–15 percent less per hour (Owen, 1978, 1979; Steuernagel and Hilber, 1984).

Employer surveys show that a prime motivation for hiring part-time and contingent workers is to reduce overall labor costs (Bureau of National Affairs, 1986). For example, temporary clerical workers directly hired by Cigna Corporation in Philadelphia are paid lower hourly rates than full-time clerical workers. Part-time airline reservation workers at the now defunct People Express and Presidential Airlines were paid half the hourly wages of full-time reservationists (Nine to Five, 1986). Supplemental or casual workers employed by the U.S. Postal Service, who comprise 10 percent of the total U.S. Postal Service labor force, receive less than half the wages of permanent workers doing the same job (Goldstein, 1990).

Part-time and contingent workers are clustered at the lower end of the economic scale. One in six part-time workers and one in five involuntary part-time workers—those who would prefer full-time jobs but are unable to find them—has a family income below the poverty level, compared to one in thirty-seven year-round, full-time workers (Levitan and Conway, 1988). More than two-thirds of the 6.4 million workers reported working and living in poverty in 1987 were employed in part-time or full-time, part-year employment compared to 29.9 percent of workers above the poverty line. The growth of these jobs has contributed to increasing income inequality in the United States. Tilly, Bluestone, and Harrison (1986) discovered that 42 percent of the growth of inequality in annual wages and salaries between 1978 and 1984 could be attributed to the growth of part-time employment and the widening gap between the earnings of part-time and full-time workers (Tilly, 1990). When workers are unable to obtain adequate full-time employment, it increases their dependency upon public welfare benefits. For instance, in 1985 33.7 percent of persons who experienced involuntary part-time employment during the year received cash or in-kind public assistance, compared to 17.9 percent of all persons with labor force experience in that year (U.S. Department of Labor, 1987).

The Federal Minimum Wage. In 1984 28 percent of all part-time workers earned the minimum wage or less compared to only 5 percent of full-time workers (Mellor and Haugen, 1986). After nearly a decade of inaction, Congress increased the minimum wage from $3.35 to $4.25 an hour

> *One in six part-time workers and one in five involuntary part-time workers has a family income below the poverty level.*

effective April 1991. However, in order to match the real value of the minimum wage in 1981, the minimum would have to be more than $5.00. In addition, the expansion of the tip credit from 45 to 50 percent of the hourly wage and the establishment of a subminimum wage for younger workers have further eroded the value of the protection offered by the minimum wage.

Business costs are an important consideration in evaluating proposals to increase the minimum wage. Equally important, however, is the weakening effect of an inadequate federal pay standard upon the entire wage structure. Tilly (1990) has shown that the lower wages of part-time workers depress the hourly earnings of full-time workers employed in the same industry. **Congress should follow the lead of several states that have raised their minimum wages to adequately reflect the changes in living costs over the past ten years.** An adequate wage floor, permanently indexed to the rate of inflation, would substantially benefit low-wage, full-time, and contingent workers alike.

Wage Parity. While most workers in the United States are covered by minimum wage legislation, regardless of the number of hours worked, there is no labor standard governing equal hourly pay for work of equal value whether part-time or full-time. The International Labour Office (ILO) (1989) reports that in Australia, Austria, Belgium, Denmark, Finland, France, West Germany, Norway, Portugal, Spain, and Sweden official labor standards and/or collective bargaining practices ensure equal hourly pay for work of equal value. More recent efforts include the development of equal pay guidelines for part-time and temporary workers in the Social Charter established to govern labor standards in a united European economy (Congressional Research Service, 1990).

In the United States, policymakers can look to the experience of labor unions who have successfully negotiated equal hourly pay rates for part-time and temporary workers performing similar jobs as full-time regular employees. Temporary auto assembly workers at the United Auto Workers (UAW) organized Mazda plant in Flat Rock, Michigan earn the same hourly amount as permanent employees (*New York Times,* 1990). Part-time workers represented by the United Food and Commercial Workers (UFCW) and the American Postal Workers Union (APWA) have traditionally enjoyed hourly wage parity with full-time workers per-

There is no labor standard governing equal hourly pay for work of equal value whether part-time or full-time.

forming the same work (Nine to Five, 1986; Goldstein, 1990). In addition, the federal government program on part-time work as well as various state employment programs preserve standards of equal pay for part-time workers performing the same work as full-time employees.

Workers who work less than full-time, whether by choice or force of economic circumstance, should not be penalized by suffering lower rates of hourly pay. Comparable worth legislation, which seeks to pay full-time workers the same wage rates as other full-time workers performing jobs with similar characteristics, is not designed to address the problem of pay inequity and work hours. **Civil rights laws should be amended to ensure that workers do not suffer discrimination in hourly pay rates as a result of their work status.** This was a policy widely adopted by manufacturing employers during World War II to attract part-time workers in wartime industries. Such policies, which were credited with reducing employee turnover and improving economic productivity, are urgently needed today.

Workers who work less than full-time should not be penalized by suffering lower rates of hourly pay.

Health Care Coverage

In Western Europe and Canada, workers and their families enjoy health care protection as a right of citizenship. In the United States, health care benefits are tied to the individual workplace, where they are keenly susceptible to economic booms and busts. They can be rolled back, expanded, or terminated depending upon the inclinations of the employer and the pressures of the market. In the current period, employers have responded to escalating health insurance costs by hiring contingent workers who receive no health benefits and by shifting these costs onto other workers and their families through higher deductibles, higher coinsurance, higher premiums, and reduced coverage. As a result, over the past five years the number of persons without health insurance has increased by 50 percent, bringing the total number of nonelderly uninsured to thirty-seven million (Employee Benefits Research Institute, 1988). The increased number of uninsured and the proliferation of self-employment, multiple-employment, and other contingent work arrangements compel policymakers to reevaluate federal tax treatment of health insurance, and to consider health care coverage strategies which transcend employer-employee relationships.

Contingent Work and the Crisis of Health Care Coverage. Three in four part-time, full-year workers don't receive health insurance directly from their jobs, compared to 88 percent of part-time, part-year workers. By way of comparison, about one in five full-time, full-year workers do not receive health care insurance through their own employment (Congressional Research Service, 1988). Fewer than 25 percent of workers employed in the temporary help supply industry work for businesses that provide some form of hospitalization or major medical plan (U.S. Department of Labor, 1988c). In many cases, temporary workers must work a minimum number of hours—often the equivalent of more than half the year—with the same agency in order to qualify (Nine to Five, 1986). Seasonal agricultural workers are the least protected group—82 percent receive no private health benefits through their employment (Congressional Research Service, 1988). And, while 82 percent of wage and salary workers are covered directly or indirectly by an employer health plan, only 46 percent of the self-employed have private health insurance (U.S. Small Business Administration, 1988).

Part-time and contingent workers often have indirect access to private health insurance through a spouse's employer-based health care plan. The Employee Benefits Research Institute (1988) estimated that approximately 26.5 percent of non-full-time workers have coverage through a spouse's employer (15.7 percent for men, 34.3 percent for women). Policymakers can take little comfort, however, in assuming that marginal workers with full-time working spouses will obtain private health care coverage. The most dramatic decline in health care coverage since 1979 has been among workers who received their health insurance through a spouse or other family member. Between 1979 and 1986, the number of worker dependents enrolled in a worker's employer-provided health care plan dropped by three million, from 34.3 to 31.4 million (Congressional Research Service, 1988). The increased number of single-parent families, comprising nearly one in four of all families with children in the United States, casts further doubt on the notion that working women, who make up the bulk of the part-time and contingent labor force, can count on their husbands for health insurance.

Congress has made some attempts to fill the gaps in employee health care coverage, but these efforts have not benefitted contingent workers. For instance, the Consoli-

Three in four part-time, full-year workers don't receive health insurance directly from their jobs.

95

dated Omnibus Reconciliation Act of 1985 (COBRA) requires employers with certain group health plans to offer continuing health care coverage to full-time employees who have been laid off or forced onto reduced work hours. However, only former full-time workers and their dependents are eligible. These families must pay the full amount of the group health plan, often prohibitive despite its lower rates relative to individual insurance, and benefits continue for only 18 months. **An immediate improvement would be to extend COBRA protection to laid off part-time workers and their dependents.** Other reforms to COBRA could include options to continue purchasing insurance from an old employer when a worker finds new employment without health care benefits. Any changes in the scope of COBRA should be accompanied by proposals to help subsidize the costs of continued coverage as well as extending the length of time this coverage is available.

Current Public Insurance Programs Offer Little Relief to the Privately Uninsured. Part-time and other contingent workers are caught between the cracks of public and private insurance systems. While private systems of health insurance are designed for permanent full-time workers and their dependents, public health insurance, including Medicaid, is designed to provide health care access to *nonworking* citizens and their families; 12.5 percent of part-time, full-year workers obtain health insurance through public sources while 27.1 percent of persons working only part-year receive publicly provided health insurance. On the other hand, 58.1 percent of nonworking adult family heads receive health insurance from public sources.

This quirk of federal Medicaid policy, which has effectively excluded low-wage workers and their families from public coverage, has been addressed in several Congressional actions to expand Medicaid coverage to children of the working poor as well as establish a new transitional Medicaid program for AFDC (Aid to Families with Dependent Children) parents moving from welfare to work. Such provisions will significantly help low-wage and contingent workers who are poor enough to qualify. However, while many states have already adopted more generous Medicaid expansions, state fiscal crises have prompted action by the National Governor's Association to block Congressional efforts to expand Medicaid, while increasing numbers of physicians refuse to serve Medicaid patients. In addition, Medicaid supports under welfare reform will pro-

> *Contingent workers are caught between the cracks of public and private insurance systems.*

tect workers and their families for only twelve months. More effective government intervention is needed to adequately protect low-wage, full-time and contingent workers.

Tax Policy. Tax laws permit employers to establish different health benefits for different groups of workers. Employees may be excluded from health plans if they have not completed one year of service, if they work less than 17.5 hours a week, work less than six months during the year, or are under the age of twenty-one. As a result, in order to economize, employers frequently exclude certain types of workers—usually non-full-time workers—from employer-sponsored health plans (U.S. Small Business Administration, 1988).

Workers without employer-provided health insurance get few tax breaks for their higher health insurance and medical costs. Families without employer-provided health coverage must purchase more expensive individual plans for which they receive fewer tax breaks. From 1954 to 1982, taxpayers could deduct a variety of medical expenses, including health insurance, to the extent that total expenses exceeded 3 percent of adjustable gross income. In 1982, under the Tax Equity and Fiscal Responsibility Act (TEFRA), the floor was raised to 5 percent and, under the Tax Reform Act of 1986, it was raised to 7.5 percent (U.S. House of Representatives, 1989c).

Prior to the 1986 tax reform, the self-employed could not deduct any of the cost of health care premiums for themselves or their employees. Tax reform enables them to deduct only 25 percent of the cost of health care premiums (U.S. Small Business Administration, 1988). By way of contrast, other employers are permitted to fully deduct the cost of health care premiums to their workers. In addition, workers are not taxed for these benefits. To increase parity between workers who receive tax-free benefits and those who do not, **Congress should increase the health care tax exemption for self-employed persons from its current level of 25 percent of the costs of health care premiums to 100 percent.**

Similarly, tax equity suggests that part-time and contingent workers who lack individual or dependent coverage through an employer should also be entitled to fully deduct the cost of their health care premiums. In most instances, individual premiums are much higher than group rates and therefore operate as disincentives for the uninsured to buy into a health care plan. This practice places unfair burdens

Tax laws permit employers to establish different health benefits for different groups of workers.

97

on other taxpayers and employers who must subsidize the care of the uninsured through higher insurance premiums and tax dollars. Even for workers with health care plans, the trend toward greater employee contributions to health care significantly strains the budgets of moderate- and low-income families who must often sacrifice dependent coverage to make ends meet. The current tax system should be more generous in allowing more of these families to deduct a greater portion of their health care expenses. **Congress should lower the floor of permissible tax-deductible medical expenses from the current level of 7.5 percent of adjustable gross income to its original level of 3 percent.** Proposals should also be developed that would offer tax credits to low-income families burdened by expensive health care premiums.

Employers should be prevented from restricting benefits to certain workers by virtue of their employment classification or work status.

Finally, employers who currently provide health care coverage should be prevented from restricting those benefits to certain workers by virtue of their employment classification or work status. **One proposal, introduced by Congresswomen Patricia Schroeder (D-CO), would require employers to offer health benefits on a pro-rated basis to part-time workers where such benefits are currently extended to full-time employees.** Another strategy would be to ensure that the repeal of Section 89 of the Tax Reform Act of 1986 include similar provisions to prevent health benefits discrimination by employee type.

Creating a Public-Private Universal Health Insurance Scheme. The above discussion offers patchwork suggestions for attacking a national health care crisis that defies small-scale solutions. The current political climate may preclude debate over the most effective solution to the health care crisis—national health insurance—which would extend comprehensive government insurance to all citizens. Instead, several leaders in government, business, and labor, including Senator Edward Kennedy (D-Massachusetts), Congressman Henry Waxman (D-California), Chrysler Corporation Chairman Lee Iacocca, and Douglas Fraser, former President of the United Auto Workers, have argued for minimum health benefits for workers and their dependents—including certain categories of part-time workers—as one strategy to improve health care coverage for the uninsured (Jacobs, 1989). While such an approach would expand labor standards to include health care insurance, many employers would continue to deny coverage to short-term and contingent workers.

For instance, under employer mandates, all regular full-time workers would be fully covered while regular part-time workers (employees who work 17.5 hours a week) would receive pro-rated benefits. Like the Schroeder proposal (mentioned above), the pro-rated benefits approach leaves significant gaps in coverage for workers who are unlikely to have the funds to subsidize the remainder of their health care costs. Similarly, the work-based approach excludes whole categories of workers who are deliberately misclassified as independent contractors, short-term hires, or temporary employees for the purpose of avoiding health care coverage costs. In addition, mandated benefits proposals overlook the problem of burgeoning health care insurance costs which burden both contingent and low-wage workers who are insured and the employers who pay for their coverage.

Congress should consider a universal health insurance scheme that provides equal access, is funded through tax revenues, and conditions coverage based upon residence rather than an individual employment relationship. A social insurance approach could promote both equity and efficiency by improving access to quality health care and by controlling its escalating costs.

Public and corporate sentiment for reforming the health care system is substantial. While the current political administration may resist more effective solutions such as national health insurance (which would essentially expand Medicare to the nonelderly as well as the elderly population), it may be possible to expand minimum health benefits to all workers and their families with significant Medicaid expansions and public-private insurance pools to ensure full coverage of individuals and their families who are outside the scope of private access. This, of course, would require dramatic shifts in public and private insurance policies: (1) employers would have to regard adequate health insurance coverage as a condition of employment rather than a cost to be avoided; and (2) federal and state governments would be required to think about Medicaid not as a welfare system for the most destitute but as a public insurance system for workers and nonworkers who fall through the cracks.

The work-based approach excludes whole categories of workers who are deliberately misclassified for the purpose of avoiding health care coverage costs.

Private Pensions and Social Security

The public and private pension system in the United States is based on an outmoded profile of the American worker: a lifelong breadwinner with an at-home spouse and children—a definition which fits less than 10 percent of the current population. For married workers whose spouses have larger pensions, longer work records, and higher earnings, economic insecurity in retirement can be minimized. But in an era characterized by dramatic changes in work schedules and family structure, it is misguided to base public policy on what we "hope" or mistakenly perceive to be available to individuals through their dependency upon someone else. When labor markets are unable to provide full-time employment for those who need it, or when women reduce their paid work time in order to resolve work-family conflicts, these workers should not be condemned to poverty in old age. The failure of government policy to address these inequities ensures that such workers end up subsidizing pension benefits for more permanently attached workers.

Coverage. Both retirement income and health care in the United States are provided by a dual public-private system in which the private components play a pivotal role. Despite regulation and special tax treatment of pension benefits, huge gaps in coverage remain. In March 1988, 16.3 percent of part-time workers were included in an employer's pension plan compared to 48.5 percent of full-time workers (Woodbury, 1989). Of the 1.3 million seasonal farmworkers, 90 percent have no pension coverage. And although Bureau of Labor Statistics (BLS) data exist on pension benefits in the temporary help supply industry, business executives in the industry report that most temporary help agencies omit pension coverage from their employee benefits packages (Fromstein, 1988). The poor coverage rates of part-time and contingent workers reflect overall declines in pension benefits in recent years. Between 1979 and 1983 the rate of pension coverage for all workers, including the self-employed, fell from 56 to 52 percent, a drop of 1.9 million persons (Andrews, 1985).

Tax Policy. Laws regulating private pensions favor full-time workers with adequate earnings and a long period of continuous service with the same employer. Under tax law, neither employers nor employees are taxed for their pension contributions—tax breaks which amounted to $52 bil-

> The public and private pension system in the United States is based on an outmoded profile of the American worker.

lion in lost tax revenue in 1990 (Moss, 1990). Yet high-wage workers with longer years of service are more likely to get these tax benefits. Consequently, the millions of contingent and other low-wage workers who are statutorily or arbitrarily denied inclusion in a company's pension plan are subsidizing the retirement incomes of richer employees.

Throughout the 1980s, there were significant tax policy reforms which strengthened pension benefits for contingent workers. Leased employees gained pension coverage as a result of the Tax Equity and Retirement Act of 1982, which requires a company with a pension plan contracting workers from a leasing or temporary agency for more than 12 months to offer pension benefits to those workers. Congress has shortened the number of years an employee must work before she or he can "vest" (earn the right to a pension benefit upon retirement) from ten to five years for single-employer pension plans. Small employers, the most frequent employers of part-time and contingent workers, have been encouraged to set up IRA-type pension plans for their workers through simplified employee plans.

Despite these gains, the persistently low coverage and participation rates of part-time and contingent workers suggest that these reforms have been inadequate in addressing the problems of pension coverage, vesting, and portability. The Employment Retirement Income Security Act (ERISA), which sets forth rules and standards for private pension plans, does not require companies to offer pensions, nor does it require that a company cover all of its workers. Employers are permitted to exclude workers under the age of twenty-one, those not working at least 1,000 hours a year, and workers covered by a collective bargaining agreement. These exclusions were limited under the Tax Reform Act of 1986. However, it is still possible for employers to arbitrarily exclude 20 percent of their employees from pension plans. Technical rules promulgated by the IRS also permit greater rates of exclusion if the nonexcluded workers represent a "reasonable classification of employees" (Moss, 1990). These tax loopholes significantly inhibit the expansion of pension benefits to part-time and contingent workers. The requirement of a year's service excludes most temporary or casual employees. Similarly, the 1,000 hour rule excludes those working, on average, up to nineteen hours per week throughout the year. In fact, there is evidence that some employers manipulate part-time work schedules to ensure that workers work less than the minimum 1,000

Tax loopholes significantly inhibit the expansion of pension benefits to part-time and contingent workers.

hours a year (Nine to Five, 1986). According to Gottlich (1990), recent ERISA reforms ordered the Secretary of Labor to promulgate rules to determine a year's worth of service in the case of agricultural workers or workers in any industry in which the customary period of employment is less than 1,000 hours. However, to date no regulations have been developed.

Pension equity demands that tax benefits be more equitably distributed. **Congress should amend the Employment Retirement Income Security Act (ERISA) to require employers who provide pension benefits to include 100 percent of their workers in a single line of business and to prohibit the exclusion of part-time workers from pension plans where full-time workers are covered.** Other initiatives for expanding pension coverage include reducing minimum service requirements for pension coverage to 500 hours in order to cover part-time workers employed below twenty hours a week year-round. Finally, Congress should require the Department of Labor to promulgate regulations defining a year of service in seasonal and temporary employment to increase the likelihood that seasonal workers meet participation and vesting requirements.

Vesting. Workers who are included in a company's pension plan may never get an opportunity to "vest" or get back their pension contributions. Traditionally, public policy on pensions has been targeted to workers with long job tenures at one company. Yet the increased mobility of American workers, especially part-time and temporary workers, suggests that lifelong employment with one firm is fast becoming the employment exception. More than half of all workers surveyed in 1988 reported job tenures of less than five years. And only about 25 percent of workers in small businesses—where part-time workers predominate—remain even three years (Employee Benefits Research Institute, 1990; U.S. Small Business Administration, 1986). Economic downturns and family responsibilities, which often break up full-time work patterns, increase the likelihood that low-wage workers will fail to vest and will therefore forfeit pension benefits.

ERISA originally mandated ten-year vesting. However, this was amended in 1986 to require companies with single-employer pension plans to allow workers to vest after five years. TEFRA now requires three-year vesting for many small companies. These reforms still leave many

> *Lifelong employment with one firm is fast becoming the employment exception.*

workers without a realistic chance of vesting. **One policy solution would be to standardize pension vesting requirements among all employers.** Frequent job changes suggest that the vesting standard under TEFRA—three years for small businesses—be extended to companies with single-employer pension plans, now under a five-year vesting rule, and multiple-employer plans, now enjoying a ten-year vesting period.

Portability. Frequent job changes, despite reforms which have increased the number of employees who have vested with several pension plans, still yield smaller returns in retirement than continuous service with one employer. Pension laws do not permit workers to carry pension credits with them to their next employer. Even when workers are able to vest, workers often receive lump sum payments in lieu of portable pension credits. They are often spent on short-term economic necessities, thereby reducing later retirement income.

While it is important to reduce the number of hours required before workers can participate in a pension plan, it is equally important to allow workers to move with their pension benefits. **Congress should examine tax strategies to promote pension portability and adopt measures which allow workers to carry pension credits with them to their next job.**

Social Security. The low rates of pension coverage for part-time workers and contingent workers increase their dependence on Social Security. Social Security, however, was meant to supplement, not supplant, retirement earnings. The varying work schedules of part-time and other low-wage workers bring lower earnings and thus, lower Social Security benefits. In particular, family members who reduce their number of paid work hours get fewer Social Security credits and thus lower benefits. Unlike caregivers in other advanced economies, such as England, who receive Social Security credits for family work, the part-time worker in the United States gets no Social Security credits for attending to his or her family responsibilities. Similarly, persons who are laid off or forced into part-time or other contingent work schedules suffer losses in Social Security credits during their time away from the labor force. On the other hand, spouses who forgo labor force participation altogether receive Social Security benefits based upon the work histories of their spouses.

Proponents of Social Security reform argue that women

Congress should adopt measures which allow workers to carry pension credits with them to their next job.

103

who leave the workforce to care for family members should not have to jeopardize future economic security (O'Grady-LeShane, 1990; Older Women's League, 1990). They argue that such workers should be provided "caregiver dropout years"—Social Security credits during years they leave the labor force to care for a family member—in order to boost their total earnings for determining Social Security benefits. Such proposals could be modified to ensure partial Social Security credits for those years a worker reduces his or her work hours rather than exiting the labor force completely. This is particularly important given the growing propensity of women to stay in the labor force upon the birth of a child, often in part-time jobs with lower earnings. **Congress should consider proposals to provide Social Security credits to workers who are forced into part-time or contingent employment as a result of economic dislocation or family necessity.** When labor markets are unable to provide workers who need full-time employment with adequate work, or when women reduce their paid work time in order to resolve work–family conflicts substantially ignored in workplace practices and public policy, these same workers should not be condemned to poverty lifestyles in old age.

> *Workers should be provided "caregiver dropout years" in order to boost their total earnings for determining Social Security benefits.*

The Special Minimum Benefit, designed in 1981 for low-wage, long-term workers, is determined differently from regular Social Security benefits. The amount of the benefit is calculated by taking years of covered employment (regardless of number of hours worked) in excess of ten but not to exceed thirty and multiplying that by a flat amount. By limiting the maximum years counted to thirty, rather than the actual number of years worked, marginal workers end up with lower monthly Social Security premiums. **The number of allowable work years (currently thirty) used for determining the Special Minimum Benefit should be changed to reflect the actual number of years worked over a worker's life.**

Targeted efforts to expand pension coverage, standardize vesting requirements, and increase pension portability, absent a more aggressive effort to universalize private pension plans, are likely to fail to adequately protect contingent and other low-wage workers in old age. In 1981, President Carter's Commission on Pension Policy recommended that Congress establish a minimum universal pension system (MUPS) to supplement Social Security. Under MUPS, employers would be required to contribute 3 percent of payroll into a defined contribution plan for each full-time employee who had been with the firm for at least one year. Vesting would have been immediate and portability would be ensured. In France, Finland, Denmark, Sweden, and Switzerland, universal schemes of employer-sponsored pensions coexist with a national system of social insurance (Social Security). In France and Finland, special private pension plans have been developed for seasonal workers such as agricultural workers and self-employed workers. In every case, employers contribute substantially to the pension fund (U.S. Department of Health and Human Services, 1986). A minimum universal pension scheme is preferable to simply increasing Social Security contributions which, as a regressive tax, would impose a significant financial burden upon low-wage workers who must pay these taxes. Similarly, the MUPS approach is an improvement over other strategies such as Individualized Retirement Accounts which are more costly for contingent and other low-wage workers to maintain, and more challenging for determining policies to ensure their portability and income adequacy. Any universal scheme must include pension protections for part-time and temporary workers who were left out of earlier congressional proposals for universal pension coverage. **Congress should investigate proposals to establish a minimum universal pension program to supplement Social Security for contingent and other low-wage workers left out of voluntary private pension plans.**

State eligibility requirements often exclude contingent workers from unemployment insurance protection.

Unemployment Insurance

The Social Security Act of 1935 created the unemployment compensation system, a social insurance program which provides temporary and partial wage replacement to jobless workers. Like Social Security, the unemployment insurance system is designed for full-time workers with strong labor force attachments. State eligibility requirements and employer practices often exclude contingent workers from unemployment insurance protection.

Coverage. Currently, 88 percent of the total civilian labor force work for employers who are covered under the federal unemployment insurance laws. Certain categories of contingent workers are excluded outright. Thirty-three states exclude casual laborers from unemployment insurance while the majority of states deny coverage to small-scale agricultural and domestic workers employed by very

105

small farmers or employers (U.S. Department of Labor, 1988b). Self-employed workers, by definition, are ineligible for coverage. Only California permits coverage of these workers on a case-by-case basis (U.S. Department of Labor, 1988b). Thirty-eight states strictly prohibit independent contractors from unemployment compensation. In many cases, however, independent contractors are actually working for one employer, yet they are denied unemployment insurance coverage while their "employer" pays no premiums (Christensen, 1986). The Internal Revenue Service estimates that 38 percent of employers misclassify employees to avoid unemployment compensation taxes as well as Social Security and workers' compensation (General Accounting Office, 1989).

State Standards. Federal standards regulating which employees are covered under a state unemployment compensation program do not distinguish between part-time, full-time, and temporary employees. Individual states, however, have full discretion over setting minimum earnings and work requirements to determine benefits eligibility. Across the United States, the average number of required weeks of work during the year is twenty. In addition, many states include a minimum earnings requirement for these weeks. Under these tests, contingent workers, particularly seasonal and temporary workers, are less likely than full-time employees to meet state eligibility requirements.

A majority of states place further restrictions on eligibility by setting a minimum earnings test for the final three months of employment of each year. Consequently, many marginal workers fail to qualify. For instance, a temporary worker earning the industry's hourly average of $6.42 for thirty hours of work a week and earning a total of $770.40 per month would fail the minimum earnings test in at least nineteen states. Similarly, a part-time worker employed up to thirty-five hours per week and earning the 1988 average hourly wage of $4.42 would fail to meet minimum earnings requirements in at least half the states. Between 1981 and 1987, in response to dwindling unemployment insurance trust funds, thirty-five states raised their minimum earnings requirement while eighteen states changed their earnings formulas for determining qualifying income over the course of a year—actions which have significantly reduced the number of unemployed workers eligible for benefits (General Accounting Office, 1988).

Once workers meet the earnings and work tenure tests of

unemployment compensation, the system further restricts benefits by limiting assistance to workers who are actively engaged in seeking "suitable" or full-time work. State case law on unemployment compensation shows that workers who restrict their hours of work to meet family care responsibilities are routinely denied unemployment insurance benefits (Commerce Clearinghouse, 1986). Ironically, a woman who forgoes paid employment to care for family members is more likely to receive unemployment insurance benefits as a dependent of a laid off spouse. Fourteen states provide dependent allowances to unemployed workers with nonworking spouses (or in some cases, very low-earning spouses) and their children. Dependent allowances are continued in full even during weeks when the primary breadwinner is only partially unemployed (U.S. Department of Labor, 1988b).

While voluntary part-time workers are often denied unemployment insurance benefits, involuntary part-time workers are better served. For instance, in nine states, workers may claim unemployment compensation when they voluntarily quit a part-time job to seek or resume full-time work (U.S. Department of Labor, 1988b). In the majority of states, "partially unemployed" workers, those working part-time involuntarily, may continue to receive benefits if weekly earnings are less than the weekly benefit amount (U.S. Department of Labor, 1988b).

Current inequities in the unemployment compensation system which disadvantage contingent workers have resulted in a profile of unemployment insurance recipients which is out of sync with the real unemployed. For instance, part-time workers, who made up 23 percent of the unemployed population in 1985, comprised just 13 percent of unemployment insurance recipients. While men make up 56 percent of the unemployed, they comprise more than 62 percent of those who receive unemployment insurance benefits. Whites comprise 81 percent of all unemployed workers yet receive more than 86 percent of the benefits. And workers with family incomes below the poverty level, who comprise over one-third of all unemployed workers, make up only one-fifth of those receiving benefits (General Accounting Office, 1988).

Updating the Unemployment Compensation System. The unemployment compensation system continues to operate according to a 1935 model of work and family life despite rapid changes in family structure, female labor

Workers who restrict their hours of work to meet family care responsibilities are routinely denied unemployment insurance benefits.

force participation, and employment patterns. Policies to reform federal and state unemployment compensation law should reflect these changes. Workers should not be penalized for their work status, nor should the unemployment compensation system encourage employers to replace their full-time labor force with irregular workers to escape unemployment compensation costs. **Developing federal standards for unemployment insurance eligibility would reduce state variability in employment protection for contingent workers.** Federal standards should include worker definitions and coverage provisions which strengthen ties between contingent workers, employers, and the state and respect the changing work lives of family caregivers. Specifically, **employers should be prohibited from misclassifying workers as independent contractors. The self-employed should be brought into the unemployment compensation system nationwide,** following the lead of California. Seasonal workers with continuous work relationships with one employer should be eligible to receive unemployment insurance benefits. In many cases these workers exhibit strong labor force attachments in the face of adverse living conditions. For example, casual workers for the U.S. Postal Service, employed primarily in rural areas, routinely return to the same post office. Farmworkers in California average three years with the same rancher (Thomas, 1985). Lastly, **voluntary part-time workers should be accorded the same unemployment compensation protection as involuntary part-timers.** Parents who seek part-time work hours to care for children are no less deserving of unemployment insurance benefits when they lose their part-time jobs than a full-time worker forced to work part-time as a result of economic conditions.

Policymakers should consider how the method of unemployment insurance financing encourages employers to deliberately misclassify employees and manipulate work hours. Under the present system, employers pay a federal unemployment payroll tax (FUTA) and a state unemployment insurance tax which varies according to the employer's experience with employee layoffs. Workers who are not defined as "regular" employees escape these counts. In recessionary periods, employers are more likely to exploit such legal loopholes in order to reduce their unemployment compensation taxes. **One remedy would be to establish a dual public-private unemployment compensation program**—a feature of several Western European systems—**in which states guarantee a minimum unemployment insurance benefit to all workers, augmented by a privately financed scheme.** Another approach is **a national "short-term compensation" program that would enable employers to reduce work hours in lieu of laying off workers and thereby reduce incentives to marginalize workers.** Short-term compensation allows employers to reduce their unemployment compensation taxes (since taxes are based on the employer's experience with worker layoffs) while workers are eligible to collect unemployment insurance benefits for hours not worked. In 1982 Congress authorized states, at their discretion, to adopt work-sharing in their unemployment compensation programs. Thirteen states now have short-term compensation programs. Congress could require implementation of such programs nationwide.

Growth of contingent employment reflects the lower quality of new job opportunities for U.S. workers.

Employment Opportunity

The growth of part-time, temporary, and other contingent employment reflects the lower quality of new job opportunities for U.S. workers, especially women and minority males. The evidence suggests that there is more involuntary part-time and temporary work than workers who want them. The failure of government and business to address the needs of working families has forced many prospective full-time workers into lesser jobs. At the same time, individuals who prefer to work less than full-time are constrained in their job choices by inadequate voluntary part-time work. Finally, workers in marginal employment often forfeit job security, opportunities for advancement, and affirmative action protection.

Contingent Work: Job Choice or Job Constraint? Over the past two decades, as increasing numbers of women with children entered the labor force, women have sought full-time work. Between 1970 and 1988, the proportion of mothers working full-time increased by 52 percent, compared to only a 14 percent increase in the proportion of mothers working part-time (U.S. House of Representatives, 1989b). This change in labor force behavior reflects the greater economic vulnerability of moderate- and low-income families in America as well as the heightened job expectations among contemporary female workers. Yet many of these workers are unsuccessful in finding the full-time employment they seek. Tilly (1990) reported that most of the increase in part-time employment in recent years can be traced to the growth in involuntary part-time work—particularly among women workers who now make up 60 percent of the involuntary part-time workforce. In recent years, women have nearly doubled their numbers as multiple jobholders, often working several part-time jobs or combining full-time employment with additional part-time hours (U.S. Department of Labor, 1989b).

> **Manual work is the fastest growing and the poorest paying segment of the official temporary labor force.**

The growth of part-time and other contingent work arrangements, when combined with the loss of better-paying, low-skill jobs in the unionized manufacturing industries of steel and auto, has created several employment problems for America's most vulnerable males. The growing preponderance of black males in blue-collar temporary employment, much of it full-time but short-term, suggests an erosion of gainful employment among the more vulnerable populations in the economy. Manual work, performed primarily by day laborers, assemblers, and freight handlers, makes up the second largest category of work in the temporary help supply industry, employing roughly one in five temporary workers (U.S. Department of Labor, 1988c). This is the fastest growing and the poorest paying segment of the official temporary labor force (Hartmann and Lapidus, 1989).

The growth in involuntary part-time employment, multiple job-holding, and casual labor indicates the failure of the U.S. economy to generate adequate full-time employment for individuals who need full-time work. **In many market economies rocked by economic change over the past two decades, reducing the standard average hours of work is viewed as an important strategy for reaching full employment and improving job quality.** For example, in 1987 German trade unions successfully negotiated a thirty-seven hour work week with German manufacturing employers, a move expected to net 100,000 more jobs in the German metalworking industries. Of the industrialized market economies, only the United States and Japan have failed to reduce hours of work—1,900 hours a year compared to 1,750 in Northern Europe (Zalusky, 1986). Since 1938, members of the U.S. Congress and the trade union movement have proposed shortening the standard work week. In 1978 and 1983, legislation was introduced that would have reduced the work week gradually to thirty-five and thirty-two hours, respectively (Kahne, 1985).

Other measures to improve the full-time job base

110

include prohibiting or limiting the use of contingent labor among federal contractors. One option would be to restrict the number of contingent workers to a specific percentage of full-time employment. Policymakers can look to the experience of unions in the manufacturing, food processing, transportation, and public sectors who have successfully won such provisions in their contracts. An innovative approach is to permit contractors to sue other contractors who underbid them where it can be shown that such contractors deliberately misclassified employees as self-employed workers to save labor costs and win contracts—a practice prevalent in the construction industry. The state of Connecticut recently enacted a law allowing such private suits.

Contingent Work and Working Families. Family members, usually mothers, are often forced into less than full-time work both by the dearth of decent job opportunities and by government and employer policies unresponsive to family needs. Nearly 35 percent of women who are working part-time or looking for work say they would work more hours if good child care were available (Presser and Baldwin, 1980). Young dual-earner couples are increasingly resorting to shift work to ensure child care coverage for their children (Presser, 1989). These problems are most severe among the one-quarter of U.S. families with children headed by a mother only. Half of these women who worked part-time in 1983 said they would rather work full-time but were constrained by the high costs and the unavailability of quality child care (U.S. House of Representatives, 1989a).

The U.S. Congress has considered a number of policy initiatives to provide support for vulnerable working families. Child care legislation has been adopted to assist low- and moderate-income families with their child care expenses and ensure additional support through new and expanded tax credits. Despite these gains, greater public intervention is required to support low-income working families and to ensure that part-time and contingent workers are eligible for new forms of assistance. For instance, one bill under consideration, the Family and Medical Leave Act, would require employers to provide workers up to twelve weeks of unpaid job protected leave for a new birth, adoption, or personal or family illness. However, this legislation requires a one-year length of service, a minimum of 1,000 hours of employment a year (or twenty hours per week), and is restricted to employers with no less than fifty workers,

> *Nearly 35 percent of women who are working part-time or looking for work say they would work more hours if good child care were available.*

leaving a significant number of contingent workers unprotected. **Several Western European welfare states provide a national system of family leave which is not conditioned by one's hours or length of employment. Policymakers should consider similar options that tie paid leaves to the unemployment insurance system and cover all workplaces as a way of expanding family leave protection to contingent workers.**

To assist our most vulnerable workers, who are often forced to combine contingent work with spells of public assistance, policymakers should acknowledge the reality that work alone is not enough to keep single parent and many two-parent families out of poverty. **Policymakers should convert current Medicaid and child care transitional benefits under welfare reform into permanent subsidies. Congress should also restore the work incentive provisions of the Aid to Families with Dependent Children program which were repealed in the early 1980s.** Both measures are needed to ensure that very low-income workers and their families will not be condemned to a future of intermittent work and long-term welfare.

Involuntary Full-Time Workers. While women in the U.S. labor force, especially mothers, have continued to enter the labor force full-time, many of these workers would prefer part-time work schedules. In addition to many mothers and fathers who would like to combine professional part-time employment with child rearing, a good number of older workers express a desire for skilled part-time work (Kahne, 1985). Tilly (1990) estimated that there are four million *involuntary* full-time workers. The lower wage, skill, and benefits levels associated with many part-time opportunities, however, severely constrain these part-time work options.

Policymakers should examine job sharing and other strategies for converting full-time work into permanent part-time employment that do not diminish full-time employment or sacrifice the working conditions of other employees. The Conference Board, in its survey of flexible work schedules, found that ninety-eight (22 percent) of the 502 companies it interviewed offered job sharing to its workers (The Conference Board, 1989). The Federal Employees Part-Time Career Act of 1978 was established to create permanent part-time positions at all levels which paid the same hourly wage as full-

> *Policymakers should acknowledge the reality that work alone is not enough to keep single parent and many two-parent families out of poverty.*

time work and provided workers with pro-rated fringe benefits. Twenty-five states, following the efforts of public sector unions, have similar programs to create better part-time employment options. Policymakers must be vigilant, however, in ensuring that alternative employment options are implemented and that opportunities extend up the job ladder. An evaluation of the federal program, conducted in 1984, found little interest on the part of federal managers to create part-time opportunities at higher levels. Only two out of seven evaluated agencies had examined vacant agency positions to determine whether part-time employment was feasible and only three agencies had established annual part-time goals and time tables (Kahne, 1985).

Phased-in retirement is an option of particular benefit to older workers. Fewer than 6 percent of private employers in a Conference Board Survey offer this alternative (Conference Board, 1989). Several Western European countries, including Sweden, Belgium, Denmark, and France, allow workers to reduce their hours of work and receive assistance from the public pension system. The program is viewed as a way to ease the transition out of the labor force and to increase the number of jobs at other levels (International Labour Office, 1989).

Equal Employment Opportunity. Men and women who choose or are forced to accept less than full-time work often forfeit job security, opportunities for advancement, and affirmative action protection. One allure of part-time and contingent work for managers is the ability to hire and fire workers without restraint, in accordance with market fluctuations. As workers largely outside the "core" of regular or permanent employment, they get none of the promotional benefits that accrue to permanent workers—including seniority rights to bid for full-time jobs. As a result, they strengthen occupational segregation by preventing women and minority group members from moving into better jobs. While private employers are more likely to engage in these practices, the increased use of subcontracting in the public sector has had particularly adverse effects on minority workers (Dantico, 1987).

The use of temporary employees can alleviate the need for compliance with federal equal employment opportunity laws (*Administrative Management,* 1986). Belous (1988) reported that in his study of fifty U.S. companies using part-time and contingent employees, only one company examined the affirmative action implications of cor-

The use of temporary employees can alleviate the need for compliance with federal equal employment opportunity laws.

porate downsizing. The federal regulations governing federal contractors under the Office of Federal Contract Compliance are silent on the question of job hours. In determining whether companies doing business with the federal government are in compliance with affirmative action, employers usually analyze how women and minority group members are utilized within the permanent full-time labor force only, ignoring other categories of workers where discrimination may be more apparent.

Some human resource specialists argue that the growth of a part-time and contingent labor force signals a declining employer commitment to career development (*Daily Labor Report,* 1988). Internal labor markets which provided avenues to career advancement within the large firm have contracted in the wake of corporate downsizing. Within small firms, where contingent work is more prevalent, internal labor markets are nonexistent (Osterman, 1988; Marshall and Osterman, 1989).

If the expansion of part-time and other contingent employment indicates a broader trend away from firm-specific training and career development, to what extent are employers and employees relying on external systems of education and training? In the case of the temporary supply industry, computer-skilled temporary workers are hired to work short-term as well as train regular employees on the use of computer systems. Although prohibited by contract, many temporary workers informally use temporary agencies to find permanent employment (Fromstein, 1988). However, the productivity interests of employers may be ill-served by a growing casual labor force that is unfamiliar with firm culture, practices, and product knowledge (Waldstein, 1989). Those workers who can get better jobs will leave their companies, thereby increasing job turnover and decreasing the pool of workers with firm-specific knowledge (Granrose and Appelbaum, 1986).

Policymakers should consider to what extent the interests of workers are best served by a private system of job training and placement which leaves many of them low-paid and unprotected while ensuring relatively high profits to employers. When employers abandon internal labor markets as a vehicle for job promotion in favor of externalizing training and job hiring, or exclude contingent workers from in-house career ladders, equal employment opportunity will continue to elude our most vulnerable workers. **In the federal sector, policymakers should direct the**

> *The productivity interests of employers may be ill-served by a growing casual labor force.*

114

Office of Federal Contract Compliance and the Equal Employment Opportunity Commission to promulgate regulations that clearly define who is an employee for the purposes of conforming to federal equal employment opportunity laws. Similarly, state and federal contractors should be prohibited or limited in their use of contingent employees following the model of manufacturing, food processing, transportation, and public sector unions that have successfully negotiated limits in the use of part-time and temporary workers within their industries (Nine to Five, 1986). The federal government should act as a model for private sector employers by repealing its ruling that temporary workers in the federal sector (which number more than 300,000) be permitted to work without benefits or seniority rights for a period of up to four years.

Congress should examine proposals to empower the U.S. Employment Service, state employment offices, or community-based organizations and non-profits to develop alternatives to commercial temporary agencies to ensure decent pay rates, continuous employment, and health and pension benefits. Surveys suggest that companies are moving toward hiring temporary or casual workers directly as independent contractors, thus lowering total wage and benefits costs and avoiding the higher markups of for-profit temporary agencies. Under an alternative system, employees would be considered permanent state or federal employees, subject to the same protection and collective bargaining rights as other public sector workers. Workers would rotate assignments in much the same manner as construction workers who receive different work assignments through union hiring halls. In some cases, nonprofit agencies have entered the day labor pool market with benefits for workers themselves. These agencies could reduce the exploitive features of the job placement process in for-profit temporary help firms (Williams, 1988).

Opening Up Public Employment and Training Programs. The growth of contingent labor, along with the increase in the number of full-time jobs which fail to provide above-poverty earnings, suggest a need to reconceptualize our notions of public employment and training programs. Programs such as the Jobs Training Partnership Act (JTPA) have historically served disadvantaged workers who are unemployed, on the assumption that paid employment would relieve economic hardship. Thus, while a contingent or full-time

The growth of contingent labor suggests a need to reconceptualize our notions of public employment and training programs.

worker may meet the income guidelines under JTPA, their employment, however inadequate, prohibits them from participating in JTPA-sponsored activities. Osterman (1988) reports that 27 percent of all female household heads and nearly 13 percent of male household heads are considered long-term, low-wage workers, yet are routinely excluded from government programs, and often public assistance, because they work. **Policymakers should recognize that many persons who are working encounter problems locating adequate employment similar to those of the unemployed and open up public employment and training programs to the working poor.**

Representing Part-Time and Temporary Workers

Much of the evidence presented in this report suggests that, in general, unionized workers receive higher rates of pay and better employment protection than do unorganized workers. For instance, in September 1989, unionized workers averaged $5.26 more an hour in wages and benefits than nonunion employees (AFL-CIO, 1989). However, unions and employers have traditionally viewed part-time and temporary workers as outside the scope of collective bargaining. In addition, labor law, which has failed to keep up to date with changing employer practices, has hindered the organization of such workers. As a result, in 1987, only 8 percent of part-time workers were represented by labor unions compared to 21.7 percent of full-time workers (U.S. Department of Labor, 1988a). This section discusses problems associated with extending collective bargaining rights to non-full-time workers and suggests strategies for improving their representation.

There are compelling cases suggesting that employers have used part-time and contingent workers to undercut union organizing drives or exact concessions during contract negotiations (Costello, 1989). For instance, in a recent organizing drive by the United Auto Workers to represent full- and part-time retail sales workers for the Hudson Department Stores in Detroit, Michigan, management increased its hiring of part-time, lesser-skilled workers and began phasing out older full-time employees with higher rates of pay and employee benefits (*Labor Notes,* 1990). During concessionary bargaining in the 1980s with the

In 1987, only 8 percent of part-time workers were represented by labor unions compared to 21.7 percent of full-time workers.

116

International Brotherhood of the Teamsters, the United Parcel Service succeeded in dramatically increasing its part-time workforce to 50 percent of total UPS workers (*Labor Notes,* 1990). After a successful organizing drive at General Electric Morristown, Tennessee's central distribution center, the company laid off most of its workforce and relocated to another Tennessee site, contracting out the distribution work (Yount and Williams, 1990). In nearly every public sector case, contracting out results in the loss of union protection for a workforce (Dantico, 1987).

Data on labor unions who do represent part-time and temporary workers suggest that unions can be instrumental in improving the job quality and career opportunities of these workers, without jeopardizing the opportunities for full-time employment. In the manufacturing sector, where unions have traditionally held greater bargaining power, unions have been successful in restricting or prohibiting the use of part-time and contingent employees (Kornbluh, 1988; Bronfenbrenner, 1988a; Nine to Five, 1986). Alternatively, unions have sought to include these workers in their bargaining units (for example, the United Auto Workers in its agreement with the Mazda Motors Corporation). In the public and private sectors, unions representing service workers have successfully bargained for restrictions on the use of part-time and contingent labor, hourly wage parity, seniority rights, pro-rated and full benefits, and opportunities for permanent employment (Engberg, 1991; Bronfenbrenner, 1988a; Appelbaum and Gregory, 1988; Nine to Five, 1986).

Legal Barriers to Unionization. Unions face tremendous obstacles to bargaining for part-time and contingent workers. Much of this difficulty derives from the complex employee classification schemes associated with the diversification of employee work schedules as well as the failure of labor law to protect contract workers. The National Labor Relations Board (NLRB) plays the major role in the determination of "appropriate bargaining units," the workplace unit in which the Board holds a representational election. The Board has been inconsistent in its rulings as to whether part-time and contingent workers should vote along with full-time employees in representational elections (Bronfenbrenner, 1988a). The approach used by the Board to define "the community of interest," from which appropriate bargaining units are drawn, often leads to false divisions between full-time and part-time or contingent

Unions face tremendous obstacles to bargaining for part-time and contingent workers.

117

employees. Under the Wagner Act (which regulates labor law in the private sector), employees' pre-existing patterns of support for union representation were highly influential in determining bargaining units. In other words, the Board might draw unit boundaries to permit a pro-union grouping to win union representation. However, the Taft-Hartley Act, passed by Congress at the behest of employers, declared it illegal for the Board to heed employee preferences in this fashion. Additionally, with the growth of temporary employment and employee leasing, the employee-employer relationship has become more complex with workers having, in effect, two employers. Taft-Hartley's ban on secondary boycotts makes it difficult for leased employees to act collectively in protest of the practices of the leasing employer (Howley, 1990b).

> ## The continued growth of part-time and contingent work challenges the very foundations of collective bargaining in the United States.

The low rates of union organization among part-time and contingent workers and the decline in union membership overall reflect the failure of labor law to keep up with changes in the employment contract. The purpose of the Wagner Act was to guarantee the right of working persons to participate in decisions that affect their working lives. One important issue for policymakers to consider is to what extent the continued growth of part-time and contingent work challenges the very foundations of collective bargaining in the United States. Part-time and contingent work contracts the base of full-time employment and thus threatens the traditional model of work underlying most labor-management agreements in the U.S. (Cordova, 1986). **Labor law must be amended to ensure that working persons, regardless of employee classification, have an effective right to organize.** One approach would be to reinstate the role of worker preferences in determining appropriate bargaining units under the law. Congress should also instruct the NLRB and comparable state agencies to include part-time and temporary workers in appropriate bargaining units according to the content of their work rather than the classification of their employment. In addition, the Taft-Hartley ban on secondary boycotts should be amended to permit collective action by subcontracted employees against a leasing employer. In the public sector, which is the most highly unionized (43.2 percent) of industry sectors, prospects may be best for unionizing part-time and contingent workers. Labor law in the federal sector and in some states provides an environment more conducive to organization than the private sector. **In reforming labor law, policymakers should examine how the NLRA regulates external labor markets operating in such industries as construction and entertainment.** In these sectors, unionized workers, like contingent workers, work intermittently and are often not attached to a particular employer; however, unlike other contingent workers, the NLRA preserves their right to collective bargaining.

Alternative Forms of Worker Representation. The enormous decline in union density in the United States over the past two decades and the historically poor rates of unionization among part-time and contingent workers suggest the need for new strategies to ensure their representation. **One approach would be to legally mandate works councils with the right to participate in management decisions related to hiring and firing, scheduling of hours, and other employment issues.** Works councils operate in Canada and in parts of Western Europe, playing a role in a variety of workplace decisions involving occupational safety and health, layoffs, and technological change (International Labour Office, 1989; Adams 1985). Unfortunately, in many of these countries, participation in works councils is denied to part-time and contingent workers (Cordova, 1986). Any move to institutionalize works councils in the United States should include these workers.

> **Works councils can be instrumental in paving the way for union representation.**

Works councils usually cover a narrow range of work issues and thus do not substitute for collective bargaining which addresses a much broader range of worker concerns. Rather, they can be instrumental in paving the way for union representation. Adams (1985) cites the Canadian experience as an example. Once workers achieve a limited set of objectives under a works council system, they may seek collective bargaining as a means to deepen their role in the enterprise.

One of the provisions of proposed reforms to the Occupational Safety and Health Act would require the selection of a safety steward in all union and nonunion workplaces with a certain number of employees. Policymakers should require these stewards to monitor the health and safety of all employees within a worksite, regardless of job classification or employment relationship. Reforms to the NLRA could authorize similar forms of representation on specific workplace issues beyond health and safety, including the determination of wages and work schedules.

Conclusion

Together, the public and private sectors should examine to what extent existing employment policies enhance or impede worker flexibility.

Contingent work is expanding in a world in which social and corporate policies adhere to rigid definitions of worker protection. Together, the public and private sectors should examine to what extent existing employment policies enhance or impede worker flexibility. Reforms must begin with the updating of our government data collection systems to get a more realistic picture of expanding work forms. The terms applied to contingent employment and the forms it takes are too varied and hidden from statistical view to enable public policymakers to respond effectively to new employment trends. Better data collection would enable researchers and policymakers to determine to what extent new work forms match particular workers' preferences for job flexibility or belie deeper structural problems in the U.S. economy.

Minimum wage laws and labor standards must be strengthened to protect marginal workers. The growth of child labor violations and the removal of protections against industrial homework suggest wrongheaded strategies to cope with labor shortages and to cut business costs. The minimum wage, which determines basic hourly wage rates for most contingent workers, must be raised well above the recent increase if we are to make such jobs more attractive than welfare or dropping out of the labor force. Where part-time work may provide genuine opportunities for middle-class workers who desire flexibility, the clustering of part-time and contingent employment at the lower end of the wage and job scale reduces decent employment prospects for the most vulnerable.

U.S. systems of social insurance—both public and private—must be revamped to include equitable coverage of part-time and contingent workers. The dramatic declines in health insurance coverage for working persons and their children should be reversed through a public-private system of universal health insurance to ensure that contingent workers, who predominate among the working uninsured, can work without fear of a child's illness or a personal injury bringing on financial ruin or increased health risks. Pensions and unemployment insurance systems which tie eligibility to full-time service can be modified to ensure that temporary and part-time workers who lose their jobs or retire are not pushed into poverty.

Part-time and contingent employment perpetuates occupational segregation by sex and race. When employers abandon internal labor markets as a vehicle for job-promotion in favor of externalizing training and job hiring, equal employment opportunity will continue to elude our most vulnerable workers. Civil rights laws should ensure that workers do not suffer discrimination in hourly pay rates as a result of their work classifications, that employers be barred from ignoring contingent workers in affirmative action "head counts," and that comparable worth legislation be extended to part-time and temporary workers.

Lastly, the contribution of the American labor movement toward improving the quality of working life and family living standards must be recognized and reinforced. Unions offer the best private remedy for bringing equity to part-time and contingent workers. Yet many of these workers are hired by management to reduce the bargaining power of labor unions. Labor law reform can open up opportunities for representing workers in nontraditional employment. Additionally, labor legislation which establishes workers' committees in all workplaces can provide a vehicle for greater communication and participation of workers in key management decisions affecting work schedules and work design.

As we rush toward the twenty-first century, the global economy, technological innovations, and demographic transformations will continue to wreak havoc with and ultimately reshape the North American labor force. Employment policies and standards which protect rather than neglect the growing numbers of contingent workers will improve labor force quality and thus strengthen the ability of the United States to perform in a volatile world economy.

Unions offer the best private remedy for bringing equity to part-time and contingent workers.

Bibliography

Abraham, Katharine G. "Flexible Staffing Arrangements and Employers' Short-Term Adjustment Strategies." National Bureau of Economic Research Working Paper No. 2617. Cambridge, MA: NBER, 1988a.

Abraham, Katharine G. "Restructuring the Employment Relationship: The Growth of Market-Mediated Work Arrangements." Washington, DC: The Brookings Institution, June 1987. Revised March 1988b.

Adams, Roy. "Should Works Councils be Used as an Industrial Relations Policy?" *Monthly Labor Review,* July 1985.

Administrative Management. "Technical Temps—A Growing Trend." February 1986.

AFL-CIO, Department of Economic Research. *AFL-CIO News,* November 13, 1989.

AFL-CIO, Executive Committee. *Report on the Evolution of Work.* Washington, DC: AFL-CIO, 1986.

Albin, Peter and Eileen Appelbaum. "The Computer Rationalization of Work: Implications for Women Workers." In Elizabeth Hagen, Jane Jenson, and Trudi Koziol, eds., *Feminization of the Labor Force: Paradoxes and Promises.* United Kingdom: Polity Press, 1988, pp. 137-52.

Andrews, Emily S. *The Changing Profile of Pensions in America.* Washington, DC: Employee Benefits Research Institute, 1985.

Appelbaum, Eileen. "Alternative Work Schedules of Women." Philadelphia: Department of Economics, Temple University, July 1985.

Appelbaum, Eileen. "Restructuring Work: Temporary, Part-Time and At-Home Employment." In Heidi Hartmann, ed., *Computer Chips and Paper Clips: Technology and Women's Employment.* Washington, DC: National Academy Press, 1987.

Appelbaum, Eileen. "The Growth in the U.S. Contingent Labor Force." In Robert Drago and Richard Perelman, eds., *Microeconomic Issues in Labor Economics: New Approaches.* Sussex: Wheatsheaf Books, 1988.

Appelbaum, Eileen and Peter Albin. "Differential Characteristics of Employment Growth in Service Industries." In Eileen Appelbaum and Ronald Schettkat, eds., *Labor Market Adjustments to Structural Change and Technological Progress.* New York: Praeger Publishers, 1990a.

Appelbaum, Eileen and Peter Albin. "Employment, Occupational Structure, and Educational Attainment in the United States: 1973, 1979, 1987." In Thierry Noyelle, ed., *Skills, Wages and Productivity in the Service Sector.* Boulder, CO: Westview Press, 1990b, pp. 31-66.

Appelbaum, Eileen and Judith Gregory. "Union Responses to Contingent Work: Are Win-Win Outcomes Possible?" In Christensen and Murphree, eds., 1988.

Baker, Helen and Rita B. Friedman. *The Use of Part-Time Workers in the War Effort.* Princeton, NJ: Industrial Relations Section, Department of Economics and Social Institutions, Princeton University, 1943.

Baron, James and Jeffrey Pfeffer. "Taking the Workers Back Out: Recent Trends in the Structuring of Employment." Graduate School of Business Research Paper No. 926. Stanford, CA: Stanford University, December 1986.

Becker, Eugene H. "Self-Employed Workers: An Update to 1983." *Monthly Labor Review,* July 1984.

Beechey, Veronica and Tessa Perkins. *A Matter of Hours: Women, Part-Time Work and the Labour Market.* Minneapolis, MN: University of Minnesota Press, 1987.

Belous, Richard S. "Contingent Workers and Equal Employment Opportunity." Paper presented at the Industrial Relations Research Association Annual Meeting, December 1988.

Belous, Richard S. "How Human Resource Systems Adjust to the Shift Toward Contingent Workers." *Monthly Labor Review,* March 1989a, pp. 7-12.

Belous, Richard S. *The Contingent Economy: The Growth of the Temporary, Part-Time, and Subcontracted Workforce.* Washington, DC: National Planning Association, 1989b.

Best, Michael. *The New Competition: Institutions of Industrial Restructuring.* Cambridge, MA: Harvard University Press, 1990.

Bilik, Al. "Privatization: Selling America to the Lowest Bidder." *Labor Research Review,* Spring 1990.

Blank, Rebecca. "The Effects of Part-Time Work on the Compensation of Adult Women." Princeton, NJ: Department of Economics, Princeton University, November 1987.

Bosch, Gerhard and Werner Sengenberger. "Employment Policy, the State and the Unions in the Federal Republic of Germany." In Samuel Rosenberg, ed., *The State and the Labor Market.* New York: Plenum Press, 1989, pp. 87-106.

Bronfenbrenner, Kate. "Organizing the Contingent Work Force." Prepared for presentation to the AFL-CIO Organizing Department. Ithaca, NY: New York State School of Industrial and Labor Relations, Cornell University, September 14, 1988a.

Bronfenbrenner, Kate. "Legal Status of Contingency Workers." Ithaca, NY: New York State School of Industrial and Labor Relations, Cornell University, 1988b.

Bureau of National Affairs. *The Changing Workplace: New Directions in Staffing and Scheduling.* Washington, DC: BNA, 1986.

Bureau of National Affairs. *The Changing Workplace: New Directions in Staffing and Scheduling.* Special Report. Washington, DC: BNA, 1987.

Business Week. "The Double Standard That's Setting Worker Against Worker." April 8, 1985.

Business Week. "Why Two-Tier Wage Scales Are Starting to Self-Destruct." March 16, 1987, p. 41.

Carey, Max L. and Kim L. Hazelbaker. "Employment Growth in the Temporary Help Industry." *Monthly Labor Review,* April 1986, pp. 29-36.

Caroll, Jaci. "Qualified Temporaries: Greater Than Ever Need." *The Office,* January 1988, p. 98.

Chollett, Deborah J. *Employer-Provided Health Benefits, Coverage Provisions, and Policy Issues.* Washington, DC: Employee Benefits Research Institute, 1984.

Christensen, Kathleen. "Pros and Cons of Clerical Homework." Testimony before the Subcommittee on Housing and Employment Opportunity, Committee on Government Operations, U.S. House of Representatives, Washington DC, 1986.

Christensen, Kathleen. "A Hard Day's Work in the Electronic Cottage." *Across the Board,* Vol. XXIV, No. 4, April 1987a, pp. 17-21.

Christensen, Kathleen. "Impact of Computer-Mediated Home-Based Work on Women and Their Families." *Office: Technology and People,* Vol. 3, 1987b, pp. 211-30.

Christensen, Kathleen. "Independent Contracting." In Christensen and Murphree, eds., 1988a, pp. 54-59.

Christensen, Kathleen. Testimony before the Employment and Housing Subcommittee, Committee on Government Operations, U.S. House of Representatives, May 19, 1988b.

Christensen, Kathleen. *Women and Home-Based Work: The Unspoken Contract.* New York: Henry Holt & Co., 1988c.

Christensen, Kathleen and Mary Murphree, eds. *Flexible Workstyles: A Look at Contingent Labor.* Conference Summary. Washington, DC: U.S. Department of Labor, Women's Bureau, 1988.

Christopherson, Susan. "The Origins of Contingent Labor Demand in Changing Production Organizations." Working Paper. Los Angeles, CA: Geography Department, University of California, December 1986.

Christopherson, Susan. "Labor Flexibility: Implications for Women Workers." Presented at the Annual Conference of the Institute of British Geographers, January 1988.

Christopherson, Susan. "Working at the Margins: The Meaning of Flexible Labor in the Changing Economy." Ithaca, NY: Department of City and Regional Planning, Cornell University, 1989.

Coates, Vary T. "Linking the Home to the Global Village." *Across the Board,* Vol. XXIV, April 1987, p. 22.

Coates, Vary T. "Office Automation Technology and Contingent Work Modes." In Christensen and Murphree, eds., 1988, pp. 29-33.

Cohen, Marcy and Margaret White. "The Impact of Computerization and Economic Restructuring on Women's Employment Opportunities." Labour Canada, Technology Impact Report, 1989.

Commerce Clearinghouse, Inc. *Federal and All-State Guide, Unemployment Insurance Reports.* Chicago: Commerce Clearinghouse, Inc., 1986.

Commission of Inquiry into Part-Time Work. *Part-Time Work in Canada.* Ottawa, Ontario: Minister of Labour, Canada, 1983.

Committee on Government Operations. "Home-Based Clerical Workers: Are They Victims of Exploitation." July 16, 1986.

Conference Board (The). *Flexible Staffing and Scheduling in U.S. Corporations.* Research Bulletin No. 240. New York: The Conference Board, 1989.

Congressional Research Service. *Health Insurance and the Uninsured: Background Data and Analysis.* Washington, DC: CRS, May 1988.

Congressional Research Service. *The Social Dimension of EC 92: The Role of Labor Policy in European Integration.* CRS Report for Congress. Washington, DC: CRS, 1990.

Cordova, Efren. "From Full-Time Wage Employment to Atypical Employment: A Major Shift in the Evolution of Labor Relations?" *International Labour Review,* Vol. 125, No. 6, November-December 1986.

Costello, Cynthia B. "The Clerical Homework Program at the Wisconsin Physician Service Insurance Corporation." In Boris and Daniels, eds., *Homework: Historical and Contemporary Perspectives on Paid Labor at Home.* Champaign/Urbana: University of Illinois Press, 1989.

Daily Labor Report. "Reduced Workweek in German Metal Working Viewed as Pattern for Other Unions." May 7, 1987a.

Daily Labor Report. May 22, 1987b.

Daily Labor Report. "West German Union's 37-Hour Work Week Should be Pattern for Others, IMF says." June 8, 1987c.

Daily Labor Report. "Greater Use of Contingent Workers Poses Questions of Firms' Commitment to Training." May 2, 1988.

Dantico, Marilyn. "The Impact of Contracting Out on Women and Minorities." In *When Public Services Go Private.* Washington, DC: AFSCME Research Department, 1987.

Day, Jeff. "Rent-A-Staff: A New Lease on Work?" *Across the Board,* Vol. XXIV, No. 7, April 1987, pp. 54-58.

Day, Jeff. "Employee Leasing." In Christensen and Murphree, eds., 1988, pp. 59-62.

Delamotte, Yves. "Workers' Participation and Personnel Policies in France." *International Labour Review,* Vol. 127, No. 2, 1988.

Dillon, Rodger L. "The Changing Labor Market: Contingent Workers and the Self-Employed in California." Senate Office of Research, July 1987.

Ehrenberg, Ronald, Pamela Rosenberg, and Jeanne Li. "Part-Time Employment in the United States." Paper presented at a conference on "Employment, Unemployment, and Hours of Work." Berlin, Germany, September 17-19, 1986.

Employee Benefits Research Institute. *Uninsured in the United States: The Nonelderly Population Without Health Insurance, 1986.* Washington, DC: EBRI, 1988.

Employee Benefits Research Institute. *Employee Benefit Notes,* February 1990.

Employee Relations Weekly. "Flexible Staffing." Special Supplement, September 8, 1986.

Engberg, Elizabeth. *Manual on Bargaining for Part-Time and Temporary Workers.* Washington, DC: Service Employees International Union, Research Department, forthcoming, 1991.

Fiamingo, Josephine. "Need a Pro? Try Temporary Help." *Office Administration and Automation,* August 1984.

Freedman, Audrey. "Jobs: Insecurity at All Levels." *Across the Board,* January 1986a, pp. 4-5.

Freedman, Audrey. "Perspectives on Employment." *The Conference Board Bulletin,* No. 194, 1986b, p. 13.

Fromstein, Mitchell. "Rising Use of Part-Time and Temporary Workers: Who Benefits and Who Loses?" Testimony before the U.S. House of Representatives, Subcommittee on Housing and Employment Opportunity of the Committee on Government Operations, 100th Congress, May 19, 1988.

Gannon, Martin J. "An Analysis of the Temporary Help Industry." Labor Market Intermediaries, Special Report No. 22. Washington, DC: National Commission for Manpower Policy, March 1978.

Gannon, Martin J. "Preferences of Temporary Workers: Time, Variety and Flexibility." *Monthly Labor Review,* August 1984, pp. 26-29.

General Accounting Office. *Unemployment Insurance: Trust Fund Reserves Inadequate.* Report to Congress. Washington, DC: GAO, September 1988.

General Accounting Office. *Tax Administration Information. Returns Can Be Used to Identify Employers Who Misclassify Employees.* Report to Congress. Washington, DC: GAO, September 1989, pp. 87-107.

Golden, Lonnie and Eileen Appelbaum. "What Is Driving the Boom in Temporary Employment? An Economic Analysis of the Determinants of Temporary Employment." Department of Economics, Temple University, for the U.S. Department of Labor, Women's Bureau, February 1990.

Goldstein, Ralph. Director of Labor Education, National Association of Letter Carriers. Interview in June 1990.

Gorham, Lucy and Bennett Harrison. "Working Below the Poverty Line. The Growing Problem of Low Earnings Across the United States." Report Prepared for the Ford Foundation and the Rural Economic Policy Program, June 1990.

Gottlich, Vicki. "Pension Equity Forum." Sponsored by the American Association of Retired Persons and the National Senior Citizens Law Center, Washington, DC, March 7, 1988.

Gottlich, Vicki. Testimony before the House Subcommittee on Retirement Income and Employment of the Select Committee on Aging, hearing on "Women in Retirement: Are They Losing Out?" U.S. House of Representatives, May 22, 1990.

Granrose, Cherylin S. and Eileen Appelbaum. "The Efficiency of Temporary Help and Part-Time Employment." *Personnel Administrator,* January 1986.

Gutchess, Jocelyn. *Employment Security in Action: Strategies that Work.* New York: Pergammon Press, 1985.

Haber, Sheldon E., Enrique J. Lamas, and Jules H. Lichtenstein. "On Their Own: The Self-Employed and Others in Private Business." *Monthly Labor Review,* May 1987, pp. 17-23.

Harrison, Bennett and Maryellen R. Kelley. "The New Industrial Culture: Journeys Toward Collaboration." *The American Prospect,* Winter 1991.

Hartmann, Heidi and June Lapidus. "Temporary Work." Washington, DC: Institute for Women's Policy Research, March 1989.

Haugen, Steven E. "The Employment Expansion in Retail Trade, 1973-1985." *Monthly Labor Review,* August 1986, pp. 9-16.

Henrickson, Susan E. and Isabel V. Sawhill. "Assisting the Working Poor." Changing Domestic Priorities Discussion Paper. Washington, DC: The Urban Institute, May 1989.

Horvath, Francis W. "Work at Home: New Findings from the Current Population Survey." *Monthly Labor Review,* November 1986.

Howe, Wayne J. "The Business Services Industry Sets Pace in Employment Growth." *Monthly Labor Review,* April 1986a.

Howe, Wayne J. "Temporary Help Workers: Who They Are, What Jobs They Hold." *Monthly Labor Review,* November 1986b, pp. 45-47.

Howley, John. "Justice for Janitors, The Challenge of Organizing in Contract Services." *Labor Research Review*, Vol. IX, No. 1, Spring 1990a.

Howley, John. Senior Public Policy Analyst, Service Employees International Union. Interview in June 1990b.

Ichniowski, Bernard and Anne E. Preston. "New Trends in Part-Time Employment." *Proceedings of the 38th Annual Meeting of Industrial Relations Research Association.* Madison, WI: IRRA, 1985.

Institute for Women's Policy Research. *Strategies to Help the Working Poor: The Union Solution.* Washington, DC: IWPR, 1990.

International Labour Office. "Flexibility in Working Time." *Conditions of Work Digest,* Vol. 5, No. 2, 1986.

International Labour Office. "Part-Time Work." *Conditions of Work Digest,* Vol. 8, No. 1, 1989.

Jacobs, David. "Labor and the Strategy of Mandated Health Benefits." *Labor Studies Journal,* Fall 1989.

Jacoby, Sanford. *Employing Bureaucracy.* New York: Columbia University Press, 1987.

Joint Center for Political Studies. "Alternative Service Delivery Systems: Implications for Minority Economic Advancement." Prepared for U.S. Department of Housing and Urban Development, April 1985.

Kahne, Hilda. *Reconceiving Part-Time Work.* Totowa, NJ: Rowman and Allanheld, 1985.

Koppel, Ross, Peter Albin, and Eileen Appelbaum. "Implications of Workplace Information Technology: Control, Organization of Work, and the Occupational Structure." *Research in the Sociology of Work,* Vol. 4, High Tech Work, 1988, pp. 125-52.

Kornbluh, Joyce. "The Contingent Workplace: Historical Perspectives on Part-Time and Temporary Workers." In Christensen and Murphree, eds., 1988.

Labor Notes. "United Auto Workers Organize Retail Workers." June 1990.

Lapidus, June. "Working 9 to 5 . . . Sometimes: The Operation of the Temporary Help Service Industry." University of Massachusetts-Amherst. Paper prepared for the Allied Social Sciences Association Meetings, Union of Radical Political Economics, December 1987.

Lapidus, June. "The Temporary Help Industry and the Operation of the Labor Market." Ph.D. dissertation. University of Massachusetts-Amherst, 1989.

Levitan, Sar A. "Labor Force Statistics to Measure Full Employment." *Society,* September/October 1979.

Levitan, Sar A. and Elizabeth Conway. "Part-Timers: Living On Half Rations." *Challenge,* May-June 1988, pp. 9-16.

Loveman, Gary and Chris Tilly. "Good Jobs or Bad Jobs: What Does the Evidence Say?" *New England Economic Review,* January-February 1988, pp. 46-65.

Mangum, Garth, Donald Mayall, and Kristin Nelson. "The Temporary Help Industry: A Response to the Dual Internal Labor Market." *Industrial and Labor Relations Review,* July 1985, pp. 599-611.

Marshall, Ray and Paul Osterman. *Workforce Policies for the 1990s.* Washington, DC: Economic Policy Institute, 1989.

Mayall, Donald and Kristin Nelson. *The Temporary Help Supply Service and the Temporary Labor Market.* Salt Lake City: Olympus Research Corporation, 1982.

Mellor, Earl and Steven Haugen. "Hourly Paid Workers: Who They Are and What They Earn." *Monthly Labor Review,* February 1986, pp. 20-26.

Mishel, Lawrence and David Frankel. *The State of Working America, 1990-91 Edition.* Armonk, NY: M.E. Sharpe Publishers, Inc., 1991.

Moss, Ann. Testimony before the House Subcommittee on Retirement Income and Employment of the Select Committee on Aging, hearing on "Women in Retirement: Are They Losing Out?" U.S. House of Representatives, May 22, 1990.

Murphey, Janice D. "Business Contracting-Out Practices: Evidence from a BLS Survey." Paper presented at the Eastern Economic Association Meetings, March 3-5, 1989.

Nelson, Ann H. "Temporary Help is Becoming a Permanent Solution." In Christensen and Murphree, eds., 1988.

New York Times. "The Two-Tier Wage System is Found to Be 2-Edged Sword By Industry." July 21, 1987, p. 20.

New York Times. "UAW Faces Test at Mazda Plant." March 22, 1990.

Nine to Five, National Association of Working Women. *Working on the Margins: The Growth of Part-Time and Temporary Workers in the United States.* Cleveland, OH: Nine to Five, 1986.

Nollen, Stanley D., Brenda B. Eddy, and Virginia H. Martin. *Permanent Part-Time Employment: The Manager's Perspective.* New York: Praeger, 1978.

Norwood, Janet. Testimony before the Employment and Housing Subcommittee, House Committee on Government Operations, U.S. Congress, May 19, 1988.

Noyelle, Thierry J. "Services and the New Economy: Toward a New Labor Market Segmentation." Conservation of Human Resources, Columbia University, 1987.

O'Grady-LeShane, Regina. Testimony before the House Subcommittee on Retirement Income and Employment of the Select Committee on Aging, hearing on "Women in Retirement: Are They Losing Out?" U.S. House of Representatives, May 22, 1990.

Older Women's League. *Heading for Hardship: Retirement Income for American Women in the Next Century.* Washington, DC: Older Women's League, May 1990.

Osterman, Paul. "Choice of Employment Systems in Internal Labor Markets." *Industrial Relations,* Vol. 26, No. 1, Winter 1987, p. 46.

Osterman, Paul. *Employment Futures, Reorganization, Dislocation, and Public Policy.* New York: Oxford University Press, 1988.

Owen, John D. "Why Part-Timers Tend to Be in Low-Wage Jobs." *Monthly Labor Review,* June 1978, pp. 11-14.

Owen, John D. *Working Hours: An Economic Analysis.* Lexington, MA: Lexington Books, 1979.

Pearce, Diana. "Toil and Trouble: Women Workers and Unemployment Compensation." *Signs: Journal of Women in Culture and Society,* Vol. 10, No. 3, 1985.

Piore, Michael J. "Fissure and Discontinuity in U.S. Labor Management Relations." In Samuel Rosenberg, ed., *The State and the Labor Market.* New York: Plenum Press, 1989, pp. 47-62.

Piore, Michael J. and Charles Sabel. *The Second Industrial Divide: Possibilities for Prosperity.* New York: Basic Books, 1984.

Plewes, Thomas J. "Understanding the Data on Part-Time and Temporary Employment." In Christensen and Murphree, eds., 1988.

Polivka, Anne E. and Thomas Nardone. "On the Definition of Contingent Work." *Monthly Labor Review,* December 1989, pp. 9-16.

Pollock, M. "The Disposable Employee is Becoming a Fact of Corporate Life." *Business Week,* December 15, 1986, pp. 52-56.

Presser, Harriet B. "Can We Make Time for Children? The Economy Work Schedules and Child Care." *Demography,* Vol. 26, No. 4, November 1989.

Presser, Harriet B. and Wendy Baldwin. "Child Care as a Constraint on Employment: Prevalence, Correlates, and Bearing on the Work and Fertility Nexus." *American Journal of Sociology,* Vol. 85, No. 5, 1980.

Progressive Grocer. "The Changing Product Mix: Labor—Growing Pains." October 1986, p. 62.

Rebitzer, James. "The Demand for Part-Time Workers: Theory, Evidence, and Policy Implications." Economic Policy Institute, Washington, DC, December 1987.

Rebitzer, James and Lowell Taylor. "A Model of Dual Labor Markets with Uncertain Product Demand." Department of Economics, University of Texas at Austin, July 1988.

Ross, Jean and Cathy Shoen. "Solutions for the New Workforce." Report prepared for September 1987 conference sponsored by Service Employees International Union and Nine to Five, National Association of Working Women, 1987.

Sacco, Samuel. "Temporary Employees Meet Needs of Business." *The Office,* May 1988, pp. 37-40.

Sansolo, Michael. "Take This Job. . . Please." *Progressive Grocer,* January 1987, p. 75.

Schmitt, Ray. *Pension Portability: What Does it Mean? How Does it Work? What Does it Accomplish?* Congressional Research Service Report to Congress. Washington, DC: CRS, 1988.

Shank, Susan. "Preferred Hours of Work and Corresponding Earnings." *Monthly Labor Review,* November 1986, pp. 40-44.

Shapiro, Ira. *Laboring for Less.* Washington, DC: Center on Budget and Policy Priorities, October 1989.

Shapiro, Ira and Robert Greenstein. *Fulfilling Work's Promise, Policies to Increase Incomes of the Rural Working Poor.* Washington, DC: Center on Budget and Policy Priorities, 1990.

Sirianni, Carmen. "Equality and the Division of Labor." *Dissent,* Fall 1985.

Steuernagel, B. and D. Hilber. "Part-Time Workers." *Review of Labor and Economic Conditions,* Vol. 11, No. 3, November 1984.

Stinson, John F., Jr. "Moonlighting By Women Jumped to Record Highs." *Monthly Labor Review,* November 1986.

Sugarman, Marge. "Employee Dualism in Personnel Policies and Practices: Its Labor Turnover Implications." Report prepared for the Region IX Employment and Training Administration, November 1978.

Sum, Andrew M. Testimony before the House Select Committee on Children, Youth, and Families. Hearing on "Barriers and Opportunities for America's Young Black Men." Washington, DC, July 25, 1989.

Terry, Sylvia Lazos. "Involuntary Part-Time Work: New Information from the Current Population Survey." *Monthly Labor Review,* February 1981, pp. 70-74.

Thomas, Robert J. *Citizenship, Gender, and Work: Social Organization of Industrial Agriculture.* Berkeley: University of California Press, 1985.

Tilly, Chris. "Half a Job: How U.S. Firms Use Part-Time Employment." Ph.D. dissertation. Cambridge, MA: Departments of Economics and Urban Studies and Planning, M.I.T., 1989.

Tilly, Chris. *Short Hours, Short Shrift: Causes and Consequences of Part-Time Work.* Washington, DC: Economic Policy Institute, 1990.

Tilly, Chris. "Reasons for the Continuing Growth of Part-Time Employment." *Monthly Labor Review,* March 1991, pp. 10-18.

Tilly, Chris, Barry Bluestone, and Bennett Harrison. "What is Making American Wages More Unequal?" *Proceedings of the Thirty-Ninth Annual Meeting of the Industrial Relations Research Association.* Madison, WI: IRRA, 1986, pp. 338-48.

Tschetter, John. "Producer Services Industries: Why Are They Growing So Rapidly?" *Monthly Labor Review,* December 1987, pp. 31-40.

Uchitelle, Louis. *The New York Times,* March 16, 1988.

U.S. Department of Commerce, Bureau of the Census. *Pensions: Workers Coverage and Retirement Income, 1984.* Washington, DC: U.S. Bureau of the Census, 1987.

U.S. Department of Health and Human Services, Social Security Administration, Office of Policy, Office of Research, Statistics, and International Policy. *Social Security Programs Throughout the World, 1985.* Research Report #60. Washington, DC: U.S. Department of Health and Human Services, 1986.

U.S. Department of Labor, Bureau of Labor Statistics. *Employment and Earnings,* Monthly.

U.S. Department of Labor, Bureau of Labor Statistics. *Linking Employment Problems to Economic Status.* Bulletin 2282. Washington, DC: U.S. Government Printing Office, August 1987.

U.S. Department of Labor, Bureau of Labor Statistics. *Industry Wage Survey: Contract Cleaning Services, August 1986.* Bulletin 2299. Washington, DC: U.S. Government Printing Office, March 1988a.

U.S. Department of Labor, Employment and Training Administration, Unemployment Insurance Service. *Comparison of State Unemployment Insurance Laws.* Washington, DC: U.S. Government Printing Office, January 1988b.

U.S. Department of Labor, Bureau of Labor Statistics. *Industry Wage Survey: Temporary Help Supply Industry 1987.* Washington DC: U.S. Government Printing Office, 1988c.

U.S. Department of Labor, Bureau of Labor Statistics. *A Profile of the Working Poor.* Bulletin 2345. Washington, DC: U.S. Government Printing Office, December 1989a.

U.S. Department of Labor, Bureau of Labor Statistics. "Multiple Jobholding Reached Record High in May 1989." *Bureau of Labor Statistics News,* November 6, 1989b.

U.S. Department of Labor, Commission on Workforce Quality and Labor Market Efficiency. *Investing in People, A Strategy to Address America's Workforce Crisis.* Washington, DC: U.S. Government Printing Office, September 1989c.

U.S. Department of Labor, Bureau of Labor Statistics. "Secretary Elizabeth Dole, Remarks Prepared for Delivery, Association of Private Pension and Welfare Plans." May 16, 1990.

U.S. House of Representatives. "Childcare: Key to Employment in a Changing Economy." Hearing before the Select Committee on Children, Youth, and Families, Washington, DC, March 10, 1989a.

U.S. House of Representatives, Select Committee on Children, Youth, and Families. *U.S. Children and Their Families: Current Conditions and Recent Trends, 1989.* Washington, DC: U.S. Government Printing Office, 1989b.

U.S. House of Representatives, Committee on Ways and Means. *Background Material and Data on Programs Within the Jurisdiction of the Committee on Ways and Means.* Washington, DC: U.S. Government Printing Office, 1989c.

U.S. Small Business Administration. *Early Jobs and Training: The Role of Small Business.* Washington, DC: Small Business Administration, 1986.

U.S. Small Business Administration. *The State of Small Business, A Report of the President, 1987.* Washington, DC: Small Business Administration, 1988.

Waldstein, Louise. "Service Sector Wages, Productivity, and Job Creation in the U.S. and Other Countries." Background Paper. Washington, DC: Economic Policy Institute, 1989.

Williams, Harry B. "What Temporary Workers Earn: Findings from New BLS Survey." *Monthly Labor Review,* Vol. 112, No. 3, March 1989, p. 3.

Williams, Randall. *Hard Labor, A Report on Day Labor Pools and Temporary Employment.* Atlanta, GA: The Southern Regional Council, 1988.

Woodbury, Stephen A. "Current Economic Issues in Employee Benefits." Paper prepared for the U.S. Department of Labor Commission on Workforce Quality and Labor Market Efficiency, September 1989.

Worsnop, Richard L. "Part-Time Work." *Editorial Research Reports,* Vol. 1, No. 22, June 12, 1987, pp. 290-99.

Yount, Linda and Susan Williams. "Temporary in Tennessee: CATS for Stable Jobs." *Labor Research Review,* Spring 1990.

Zalusky, John L. "Labor's Concern with the New Directions in Staffing and Scheduling." In *The Changing Workplace.* Washington, DC: Bureau of National Affairs, 1986.

Index

E

Earnings. *See* Wages
Education, 7
Efficiency, 36
Employee Benefits Research Institute,
    22, 95
Employee leasing firms. *See* Temporary
    Help Supply
Employee Retirement and Income
    Security Act (ERISA), 38, 78, 101,
    102
Employment. *See* Contingent
    employment; Direct hires; Labor;
    Part-time employment; Temporary
    employment
Engineering labor market, 59–60
Equal employment opportunity, 76,
    109–16, 121
Equal Employment Opportunity Act,
    77
Equal Employment Opportunity
    Commission, 115
Equity, 36
ERISA. *See* Employee Retirement and
    Income Security Act

F

Fair Labor Standards Act, 77
Family
    income, 21–22, 36, 92
    parental leave, 39
    responsibilities, 72, 103
    working, 111–12
Family and Medical Leave Act, 111–12
Federal Employees Part-Time Career
    Act of 1978, 112
Federal unemployment payroll tax
    (FUTA), 108
Firms, 7–8
    employment practices of, 73–74
    risks of contingent employment, 76

Flexibility, 38–39, 81–82, 120
Full-time work, involuntary, 25, 33–34,
    36, 112
FUTA. *See* Federal unemployment
    payroll tax

G

Golden, Lonnie, 72, 74
Gottlich, Vicki, 102

H

Hazelbaker, Kim L., 59
Health insurance, 94–99
    as a benefit, 22–23
    as a benefit for temporary workers,
        56–57
    and contingent employment, 95–96
    declines in, 120
    and flexible arrangements, 81–82
    in manufacturing, 69
    universal, 39
Hewitt Associates, 23

I

Ichniowski, Bernard, 26
ILO. *See* International Labour Office
Income, family, 21–22, 36, 92
    see also Wages
Independent contractors, 68, 106
Industrial help workers, 54
Industrial labor model, 73–74
Information technology, 9–11
Insurance industry, 32
    see also Health insurance
International Labour Office (ILO), 37,
    93

Temporary Help Supply (THS), 3,
47–60, 74–75
  benefit coverage for, 56–58
  characteristics of workers, 50–52
  employment, 48
  federal regulation for, 77–78
  growth trends in, 71–72
  reasons for use of, 63
  wages, 56
  work hours, 52–56
  work settings, 58–60
Temporary worker usage
  by benefit level, 65
  by firm size, 64
  by industry, 66
  by stability of employment, 65
THS. *See* Temporary Help Supply
Trade industry, 28–30
Training programs, 115–16
Travelers Corporation, 67–68
Travelers Insurance Company, 78–79
Turnover rate, 34, 114

U

Uchitelle, Louis, 58
Unemployment, 26–27
Unemployment insurance, 37, 78,
105–9, 120
  coverage, 105–6
  state standards, 106–7
  updating system, 107–9
Unions, 6, 40, 111, 116–19
  barriers to organization, 117–19
  busting, 8
  and collective bargaining, 79
  decline in power, 74

Unions (*con't*)
  and wage parity, 93–94
United Auto Workers, 6
United States
  part-time employment in, 40
  social insurance in, 37–38

V

Vacation pay, 58
Vesting, 102–3

W

Wages, 38, 69, 91–92
  of direct hires, 62
  gap in, 21–22, 27–28, 40, 91
  parity, 93–94
  of temporary workers, 56
  see also Minimum wage
Wagner Act, 118
Women, 71, 75
  and child care, 111
  as disproportionate part–time
    workers, 2–4, 17–19, 50
  and employment opportunity,
    109–10
  involuntary part–time employment,
    36
  wages, 56
Worker choice, 49, 77
Worker preferences, 71, 118
Worker safety, 77–78
Working families, 111–12
Works councils, 119
Work week reduction, 110

Eileen Appelbaum is the Associate Research Director at the Economic Policy Institute. She has authored several books and published numerous articles on labor economics, women's employment, growth of contingent work arrangements, impacts of information technology on employment and labor skills, and macroeconomics and financial markets. Dr. Appelbaum has published extensively and currently ranks 24th among academic women economists nation-wide according to citations to her published work as tracked by the *Journal of Economics and Business.*

Françoise J. Carré is a doctoral candidate in the Department of Urban Studies and Planning at the Massachusetts Institute of Technology. Her research concentrates on contingent work in the United States and France.

Virginia L. duRivage is a social policy consultant for EPI. Before her work with EPI she worked extensively on the employment and economic concerns of low to moderate income families for the U.S. House of Representatives Select Committee on Children, Youth, and Families. She is the former Associate Research Director of 9 to 5, the National Association of Working Women. She is the author of an EPI Briefing Paper by the same title as her chapter and two studies, *Working at the Margins: Part-time and Temporary Workers in the United States* and *Computer Monitoring and Other Dirty Tricks,* distributed by 9 to 5.

Chris Tilly is Assistant Professor of Policy and Planning at the University of Massachusetts-Lowell. His recent research has explored part-time work, income inequality, poverty, and discrimination. He is the author of an EPI study of the same title as his chapter in this book, from which his chapter was excerpted.

The Economic Policy Institute was founded in 1986 to widen the debate about policies to achieve healthy economic growth, prosperity, and opportunity in the difficult new era America has entered.

Today, America's economy is threatened by stagnant growth and increasing inequality. Expanding global competition, changes in the nature of work, and rapid technological advances are altering economic reality. Yet many of our policies, attitudes, and institutions are based on assumptions that no longer reflect real world conditions.

Central to the Economic Policy Institute's search for solutions is the exploration of the economics of teamwork—economic policies that encourage every segment of the American economy (business, labor, government, universities, voluntary organizations, etc.) to work cooperatively to raise productivity and living standards for all Americans. Such an undertaking involves a challenge to conventional views of market behavior and a revival of a cooperative relationship between the public and private sectors.

With the support of leaders from labor, business, and the foundation world, the Institute has sponsored research and public discussion of a wide variety of topics: trade and fiscal policies; trends in wages, incomes, and prices; the causes of the productivity slowdown; labor market problems; U.S. and Third World debt; rural and urban policies; inflation; state-level economic development strategies; comparative international economic performance; and studies of the overall health of the U.S. manufacturing sector and of specific key industries.

The Institute works with a growing network of innovative economists and other social science researchers in universities and research centers all over the country who are willing to go beyond the conventional wisdom in considering strategies for public policy.

The research committee of the Institute includes:

Jeff Faux—EPI President
Lester Thurow—Dean of MIT's Sloan School of Management
Ray Marshall—former U.S. Secretary of Labor, currently a Professor at the LBJ School of Public Affairs, University of Texas
Barry Bluestone—University of Massachusetts-Boston
Robert Reich—JFK School of Government, Harvard University
Robert Kuttner—Author; columnist, *New Republic*, and *Business Week*; co-editor, *New Republic*

EPI Reports, Working Papers, Briefing Papers, and Seminars are distributed by *Public Interest Publications*. For a publications list or to order, call 1-800-537-9359.

Other **EPI books** are available from ME Sharpe at 1-800-541-6563.

For additional information, contact the Institute / 1730 Rhode Island Ave., NW, Suite 200 / Washington, DC 20036 / 202-775-8810.